The
MOSAIC
MYTH

The
MOSAIC
MYTH

The Social Integration
of Newcomers to Canada

DOMENIC DIAMANTE

DUNDURN
PRESS

Publisher: Kwame Scott Fraser | Acquiring editor: Kathryn Lane | Editor: Wade Hemsworth
Cover designer: Karen Alexiou
Cover image: amtitus/istock.com

Library and Archives Canada Cataloguing in Publication

Title: The mosaic myth : the social integration of newcomers to Canada / Domenic
    Diamante.
Names: Diamante, Domenic, author.
Description: Includes bibliographical references.
Identifiers: Canadiana (print) 20230445330 | Canadiana (ebook) 20230445381 | ISBN
    9781459753075 (softcover) | ISBN 9781459753082 (PDF) | ISBN 9781459753099 (EPUB)
Subjects: LCSH: Multiculturalism—Canada. | LCSH: Social integration—Canada. | LCSH:
    Immigrants—Canada.
Classification: LCC FC105.M8 D53 2023 | DDC 305.800971—dc23

We acknowledge the support of the Canada Council for the Arts and the Ontario Arts Council for our publishing program. We also acknowledge the financial support of the Government of Ontario, through the Ontario Book Publishing Tax Credit and Ontario Creates, and the Government of Canada.

Dundurn Press
1382 Queen Street East
Toronto, Ontario, Canada M4L 1C9
dundurn.com, @dundurnpress

Contents

A Note from the Editor

This book was inspired by events and dynamics in Canada in the late 1970s and early 1980s, when there was hot debate on questions of ethnic identity, Canada's relationship to the Commonwealth, and the qualities that defined being Canadian. Canada had recently come through the divisive 1980 Quebec referendum and Prime Minister Pierre Trudeau's government was fresh from repatriating Canada's Constitution, including a new Charter of Rights and Freedoms.

It was a time of great debate regarding the best way to approach the integration of newcomers to Canada, and to balance the independence and character of ethnic groups within the existing framework of society.

Today, nearly forty years after this book was first drafted, these issues are still being debated, but in new contexts and with new groups of immigrants and refugees settling in Canada, including people escaping famine and war in East Africa, bloody conflict in Central America, and wars in Iraq, Iran, Afghanistan, the former Yugoslavia, Syria, Ukraine, and elsewhere.

This book is deliberately presented in its original context, including language and events contemporary with the period in which it was first written, to preserve its authenticity and to frame these ideas in a way that is readily comparable to the events and circumstances that have developed since that time.

To that end, phrases in use at the time of the first writing remain intact here, even though some, such as "Third World," have changed since then, as understanding and concern for the fairest forms of representation have developed. In particular, the term "Native" has, given growing understanding and respect, since broadly been replaced by the more inclusive term "Indigenous." While the author understands, respects, and celebrates this change, this book uses the language of the time as it appeared in the original manuscript, to maintain consistency with the period.

— Wade Hemsworth, April 2023

Introduction

In November 1982, an important and divisive municipal election took place in Toronto. Besides choosing among the typical municipal issues, voters in one of Canada's most ethnically diverse cities were asked to select school-board candidates who would consider controversial reforms to the educational policies of those school boards.

Proposed reforms to educational policies do not typically spark visceral animosity, but these did. On the table was cultural identity, as expressed through the debate over offering "heritage language" education.

Depending on the result of the election, trustees could be given a mandate to begin implementing the teaching of the heritage languages of their students — not optional after-school classes, as had been offered to that point, but core classes during regular school hours. Heritage language students would be taken out of classrooms they shared with "non-ethnics" and moved to other classrooms to receive instruction in their heritage languages. In time, this first phase would be followed by a second, which would see students learning other subjects — such as mathematics, history, and geography — in their heritage languages. As a subject, English would in fact become for them a second language, and French, if desired, a third language. But what was at stake was much more than the language of instruction.

The issue of which languages to use for the education of Toronto's school population evoked heated, emotional responses during the campaign. Voters either embraced the changes or vehemently rejected them. This significant shift in the approach to education reflected what had been fomenting in the broader social, political, and economic landscape of Canadian society and across the world.

As international trade expanded after the Second World War, new routes and infrastructure emerged to serve the new growth. This changing world of greater international commerce prompted a corresponding shift in the world's population, one that is still occurring. People move to where there are jobs, which is typically in the centres of commerce. The world was becoming more interconnected and a change of attitude regarding culture was surfacing and taking hold of people's ways of relating to the "other." The dominant view had been that newcomers should assimilate and adopt a country's cultural views and norms. Immigrants should eschew their heritage, assimilate, and let go of their old-fashioned ways.

The assimilationist outlook has become anachronistic; it is no longer seen as an appropriate way of integrating immigrants. As the world has become increasingly connected, assimilationist theories of social integration and others, such as the melting pot, have become increasingly dated. Canada, within the orbit of developed Western countries and with an important need for continued economic growth, has changed its perspective on the integration of newcomers. The changed approach was also, or mainly, prompted and facilitated by two other issues that have plagued Canada from its incipient stages: the role of the province of Quebec and the recognition of the fundamental importance of the Native population.

INTRODUCTION

In the 1960s, Canadian cities and rural communities were teeming with numerous and varied ethnic populations doing exactly what Canada needed and what the government had hoped for by encouraging immigration: a large labour force that could work in its expanding industries, increase agricultural production, and build appropriate infrastructure for the growing country. But cultural institutions did not keep up with the changes. The harmony of society was threatened and disrupted by the political activism of French Canada demanding separation, by the tacit demands of some ethnic organizations for seats at the table, and by ethnic incursions into the spheres of economic influence. Something had to be done. In 1963, the Royal Commission on Bilingualism and Biculturalism (RCBB) was established to deal with these issues. In 1971, on the Commission's recommendation, Prime Minister Pierre Trudeau led the creation of a policy of multiculturalism. The policy largely reflected the spirit of cultural pluralism. Still, it is worth noting that while policy-makers did adopt most of the Commission's recommendations, some of the underpinnings were overlooked, which led to unintended political consequences. Nonetheless, the policy reflected the new views of the times, including new models for the cultural integration of newcomers and responses to some of the demands from the ethnic communities. A social shift occurred, reflecting the discourse of the nation and taking hold of the people's collective imagination. The model has since become more than just a description or metaphorical label for Canadian society. It has become an ideology: the ideology of the mosaic. By "ideology," we mean a construct of ideas, a vision of society that intends to effect changes in the social habitat — in our case, the manner of integrating newcomers into Canadian society. It provided an alternative to the assimilation and melting pot theories. It is a new paradigm, a different vision of Canada that demands attention and motivates political and social activism.

The ideology of the mosaic has moved far from the theory of cultural pluralism and the central and basic idea of the relativity of culture, which holds that a culture is relevant, important, and pertinent to the particular people who have developed, sustained, and cherished it within their own socio-economic and political context. This valid concept becomes abstracted and loses pertinence in the ideology of the mosaic. Culture has been taken out of a particular social and historical context and become asocial and ahistorical.

The metaphor of the mosaic describes this theory well, and from our perspective, in a negative way. A mosaic is a fixed schematic design with no flexibility or capacity for movement. It has a persistence in time, character, and substance. It is representative of a specific period of cultural and historical circumstances and of a definite design. In fact, the ideology of the mosaic has emerged as a force that could indeed prevent the cultural, spatial, and economic fluidity of ethnic populations; under its strictures, heritage, culture, and language could become constraints meant to keep them in their place and prevent social or economic mobility.

Cultural pluralism is not intended to operate this way. It is malleable, ebbing and flowing in keeping with changing times and characteristics determined by historical circumstance, including social events that at times evolve beyond any form of control. Cultural pluralism in Canada is an observable fact that shapes and reshapes itself. Culture itself, whether as a value system or as a behaviour, is malleable. It can retain some original characteristics while responding to social and historic developments. But an ideology can unite and divide. The ideology of the mosaic is doing just that. It has evoked social and political activism on both sides of the divide. Its repercussions for society, whether positive or not, will determine how well it holds and reveal its validity when compared with its stated objectives.

We want to analyze the ideology of the mosaic that has given structure to the theory. We want to deconstruct this theory by looking at the assumptions that form its armature. Theoretical formulations have validity only if their assumptions are historically, politically, and socially sound. Without sound assumptions, policies can never align with their corresponding societies.

The theory of the mosaic features assumptions about immigration, ethnicity, and ethnic culture that do not correspond to the historical and social realities of ethnic groups in Canada. It rests on three fundamental assumptions: that we are all immigrants in Canada, that all Canadians are ethnics whose national identity can be hyphenated, and that ethnic culture is permanent and unchanging. In this book, we analyze these assumptions and confront them with the actual historical, cultural, and political essence of Canadian society relative to the ethnic social integration process.

Chapter 1

The Social Integration of Newcomers to Canada

Immigration is an integral part of Canada's history. More than one-third of Canada's population derives from a non-French or a non-British ancestry, whether this is viewed positively or not. Canada has pursued immigration policies that have brought people from all corners of the world. Canada's forests and lakes — which, until a few hundred years ago, had known only Native populations — have since witnessed people from almost all the world's nationalities and races, all coming — at least metaphorically — to hew their wood and draw their water.

Still, the policies that have drawn millions of immigrants to the country have not been met with unanimous approval. They have sparked heated debates and more than once been the focus of election campaigns. Of the myriad views regarding immigration, two opposing ideas came to dominate, each seeking to influence the number and quality of people entering Canadian territory.

On one side were those promoting a large influx of people needed to build the economy and populate the largely uninhabited land. The newcomers would provide a reservoir of workers to take jobs that Canadian workers did not want. Political and economic elites in Canada demanded a larger, cheaper workforce. As Donald Avery points out in his book *Dangerous Foreigners*, "Only the European workers seemed prepared to face the irregular pay, high accident rates, crude living conditions and isolation that characterized the workforce in the expanding parts of the Dominion's economy."[1]

On the other side were those who wanted to curtail immigration, fearing that a great influx of people from different cultural backgrounds would diminish Canada's culture and erode its character. In September 1906, an editorial in *Saturday Night* stated openly that "this is a white man's country and white man will keep it so. The slanted eye Asiatic, with his yellow skin, his unmanly humility, his cheap wants would destroy the whole equilibrium of industry. He would slave like a Nubian, scheme like a Yankee, hoard like the proverbial Jew."[2] By 1924, the mood had not changed. In an article appearing in *The Toronto Telegram* of that year, the same racist ideas were expressed regarding keeping those who were different out of the country: "An influx of Jews puts a worm next to the kernel of every fair city where they get a hold. These people have no national tradition.... They engage in the wars of no country, but flit from one country to another under passports changed with chameleon swiftness, following up the wind to the smell of a lucre."[3]

The Canadian government found itself in the awkward position of reconciling these two conflicting views. The pressures from those seeking to expand the Canadian economy with the help of immigrants could not be dismissed. At the same time, political parties wanting to gain or remain in office could not disregard the significant portion of voters who wanted to restrain immigration. Placed between these seemingly irreconcilable views, governments generally served the interests of the first by adopting, with some interruptions, policies of massive immigration. At the same time, they made efforts to reassure the public that the immigrants would abandon their ways and be absorbed into the Canadian way of life.

As political realities pushed politicians to meet the needs of a growing economy while also placating anti-immigration views, the goal and model of assimilation came to the rescue.

The Theory of Assimilation

Assimilation provided reassurances that immigrants would lose their "strange ways," shed their foreign coats, and adopt the customs of the majority population. From the nineteenth century, when mass immigration began, until the official declaration of multiculturalism in 1971, the Canadian government sought to assimilate immigrants into Canada's cultural and linguistic traditions.

This was meant to render innocuous the effect that mass immigration could have on Canadian culture and its institutions. It was hoped it would curb the anti-immigrant views of the host population toward newcomers who displayed different traits and neutralize the distaste for political groups and economic lobbyists pushing for more immigration.

In fact, in 1919, as reported in *The Lethbridge Herald*, the Daughters of the Empire passed resolutions for a Canadian campaign "to propagate British ideas and institutions," "to banish old-world points of view, old-world prejudices, old-world rivalries, and suspicion and to make new Canadians 100 percent British in language, thoughts, feelings, and impulse."[4] In other words, they wanted whatever cultural baggage the immigrants might be carrying to be emptied and filled with Anglo-Canadian cultural goodies. Government policies with an assimilationist perspective were expected to fulfill this task.

Pressures on the immigrant to conform to Anglo-Canadian cultural norms were relentless and psychologically devastating for those who faced them. Assimilation presented a conflict for the individual immigrant who wanted to establish himself firmly in

Canadian society without relinquishing his cultural background. It created divisions between immigrant parents, for whom total acceptance of new cultural norms was difficult, and their children, who underwent a socializing process in Canadian schools and other institutions of the land. Furthermore, it generated conflict within the children themselves, who wanted to be like other Canadian children but also wanted to respect their parents and their ways.

John Marlyn, in his novel *Under the Ribs of Death*, illustrates this conflict quite succinctly. In a dialogue between the immigrant father, who wants to continue speaking and behaving as a German, and his son, who wants to confront his "foreignness" in school and be like the others, the child argues his case:

> "The English," he whispered. "Pa, the only people who count are the English. Their fathers get all the best jobs. They are the only ones nobody ever calls foreigners. Nobody ever makes fun of their homes or calls them 'baloney eaters' or laughs at the way they dress or talk, nobody." He concluded bitterly, "Because when you're English, it's the same as being Canadian." In response to what appears to him as useless rhetoric of the father, "It is meaningless to call anyone a foreigner in this country. We are all foreigners here." The child resolves to get rid of all his foreign traits. Someday he will grow up and leave all this, he thought, leave it behind him forever and never look back, never remember his dirty, foreign neighbourhood and English gang who chased him home from school every day. He would forget how it felt to wear rummage sale clothes and be hungry all the time, and nobody would laugh at him again, not

even the English, because by then he would have changed his name and be working in an office as the English did, and nobody would be able to tell that he had ever been a foreigner.[5]

The goal of making immigrants 100 percent British, in the case of this young boy, would have been achieved.

Although this is a fictional account of the pressures of assimilation on a young boy and his father, the reality is not far from it. Research by the Canadian Institute of Cultural Research and published in *Ethnic Change of Name* shows that the anglicizing of names is more widespread than it might appear. Case histories reported in the study provide a clear understanding of what motivated this phenomenon.

The first case is of a Mr. A, a fifty-year-old lawyer in Toronto.

Mr. A spent his growing-up years and youth in a city in western Canada. He reported with humour how, in his dating years, he and his friends had adopted Anglo-Saxon movie star names on Saturday afternoons spent [pursuing girls] in his father's car. "As long as they did not know we had a 'ski' on the end of our names," he said, "everything was fine." One afternoon, however, his attempts to eliminate the "ski" impressions were foiled: the young lady he had met that afternoon happened to look in the glove compartment of his father's car and, much to her amazement, found a Polish newspaper there. Mr. A reported that the good impression he had made until then, with the help of his assumed Anglo-Saxon name, was crushed. Upon finding that Mr. A came from the "other side of town," his young friend vanished with considerable speed. Mr. A stated that in his student days, it was much easier to obtain a minor job if he stated an Anglo-Saxon name on his application. It was not until he was in his thirties, however, that a company, of which he was to become a director, requested that he changed his name legally.[6]

The second case history deals with a Mr. B who, for different reasons, used a pseudonym.

Mr. B, a native of Latvia, is now a maintenance worker in Toronto. In Latvia, he had been a law student. When he immigrated to Canada, he found that his training in Latvia would not permit him to become a lawyer here. Consequently, he established his own carpentry business, but when he injured his back in an accident, it became evident to him he would have to abandon his business. After the accident, he went to the civil service to try to get a job "that I would like and would be interesting." He was told there wasn't anything for him. He reported having asked if it would make any difference if his name was Mr. Smith. He says, "In Canada, it matters not what you know, but who you know. It is very difficult for one who wanted to be a lawyer, to sweep floors." Mr. B changed his name because he did not want his son to experience any of the difficulty he had. He stated that he had some regret about losing his Latvian name but could not afford to be sentimental when his son's future was at stake. "The change will not make any difference to me now, but it will mean everything to my son," he said.[7]

The third case deals with a Mr. C, who was a Canadian born of Ukrainian parents and did not have strong links to the Ukrainian community.

He is quoted as saying that "during his childhood English was the language usually spoken in his home; some Ukrainian was spoken but he says his understanding of that language is very limited." He said that he decided to change because of the business inconvenience of having your name constantly misspelled and mispronounced. Further, he said, "I get tired of people asking me where I was born, when I was born right here in Canada." He added, "When you have a foreign name, it is very difficult before people get to know you well; after they get to know you, it's all right, but meanwhile it is very inconvenient." He felt that a change of name was necessary for him now that he was embarking on a business career and tracking toward marriage. He said, "All of a sudden you are no longer a foreigner when you change your name; this is especially important in business." For Mr. C, there was no inner conflict involved in change of name because he said, "I've never felt like a Ukrainian, and I've never done many Ukrainian things; I just happened to be born with a Ukrainian name, that's all."[8]

Yet, as these processes were taking place, including all the drama they created for individuals, the Anglo establishment did not view such developments positively. In fact, while the Daughters of the Empire exhorted immigrants to become "100 percent British, in language, thought, feeling and impulse," they also protested against foreigners taking British names. Clearly, the Daughters of the Empire did not want full assimilation. They made a conscious effort to have the immigrants become like them, but also to be kept apart and, possibly, on the periphery. The Daughters of the Empire were fully aware that once European immigrants — and, later, their daughters and sons — had mastered the language, adopted Anglo cultural norms, and changed their names, they could no longer be distinguished from Anglo-Canadians. Once that transformation was complete, they could no longer be stopped from entering the power structure of the system and participating equally in society, a possibility they found distasteful and threatening. The Daughters of the Empire would have been horrified if, for example, the young European man who had changed his name had continued dating the English-Canadian woman and, God forbid, ended up marrying her.

If we take a broad look at the policy of assimilation, we can see that in some ways, it has been successful. We know some immigrants dropped their cultural baggage and adopted Anglo-Canadian ways. The changing of names is an extreme illustration of this phenomenon. However, it is also true that the policy did not, in other ways, fully achieve its goals. Many immigrants chose not to shed their foreign coats and instead continued to express their diversity. The fact that many communities openly and proudly express their ethnicity is a clear example of this policy's failure.

The existence of these communities is clearly evidence of a policy that, as we have seen, featured contradictory objectives and treated newcomers in a discriminatory, even racist fashion. In fact, the policy can be said to have actually pushed immigrants together into separate communities that would permit the preservation of some aspects of their former cultural lives. The policies directed to assimilating new arrivals did not take into account that immigrants had come to participate in the development of their new country as unique individuals with a particular view of life and cultural norms of their own. Importing people into a country is not the same as importing goods. Immigrants arrive with well-formed cultural identities, and even those who are willing to neglect or abandon their backgrounds find it is not so easily done. All this must be taken into account in the process of settling newcomers.

Any policy of integration must also consider the cultural and social dynamics of bringing in a massive number of people from other places. It must consider the immigrants' backgrounds, the social relations that will develop from their new roles in the labour force, and their relationships with other immigrants and the broader population. To believe that immigrants will simply accept that their homeland cultures are inferior and willingly abandon them is simplistic, arrogant, ethnocentric, and unfair.

Despite these shortcomings, for nearly one hundred years assimilation has been Canada's dominant model for socially integrating immigrants. The fact that it left so many of them feeling degraded did not appear to matter. Their culture shock, their identity crises, their economic hardships, and their experiences of discrimination at work and outside work were all pushed aside. The idea was that in the process of assimilation, these problems would vanish. In theory and in practice, assimilation failed to consider the problems immigrants faced from the moment of their arrival. It also failed to recognize that immigrants already had cultural identities and, in most cases, were not willing to discard them as if they were old clothes.

Assimilationists believed in the dominance of one culture over others in a way that at least bordered on racism, if unconsciously.

Essentially, they held the view that once immigrants came into contact with Anglo-Canadian culture, they would willingly adopt it as their own. In this way, the theory of assimilation falls more within a liberal ideology than a racist one.

The Melting Pot

The theory of assimilation first began to be questioned and challenged in the United States, where programs for the social integration of immigrants were based on principles similar to those of Canada. There, alternatives began to emerge, starting with the theory of the melting pot and, later, cultural pluralism. In fact, the common metaphor for integrating immigrants into American society is the melting pot.

This theory caught and for a long time held the imagination of those seeking a more humane alternative to the brutal process of assimilation. Under the melting-pot concept, American culture would develop in keeping with the interplay between what had already existed and the cultures contributed by immigrants to the U.S. In the melting-pot model, American culture was not to be regarded as static, but dynamic — evolving as new cultural ingredients were introduced to the cauldron. As Jim Cummins and Harold Troper describe it, "The melting pot envisioned a dynamic process of societal accommodation of new culture elements. Immigrants did not simply become Americans. The melting pot continually introduced new elements into the American community to create a constantly changing American character. American culture, by definition, remained open to further changes as new groups added to the whole. The American man was thus not an immutable model, but a dynamic personality in flux, a constantly evolving ego."[9]

This was certainly an ideal to which both the existing American population and the growing waves of immigrants could aspire.

What must not be forgotten is that during the nineteenth century and much of the twentieth, the U.S. was in a period of phenomenal structural growth. Immigrants were desperately needed to fill the vast expanses of its sparsely populated land. They were needed to enable industrial growth and to provide an internal market for manufactured goods. This demanded a larger population. An attractive approach to social integration would provide an incentive, above and beyond the material benefits, for immigrants to settle permanently on American soil.

Just as important, American society was forging its cultural identity from within itself, not importing one from abroad. Unlike Canada, the U.S., as a nation state, had forcibly separated itself from England's imperial power by armed revolution. This demanded that the economic and social order be re-established in keeping with new, independent national interests. American culture and identity could not rely on a "back-home" model; they had to be fashioned on American soil. Ultimately, the new nation endured a civil war, which demanded a new post-colonial identity that could politically unite the North and the South, the East and the West, including the culturally and racially diverse populations within them. The melting pot proved to be a durable metaphor: American society would become an amalgam of all the world's cultures and, in so doing, create a unique new culture of its own.

This ideal was at least partly realized, but unfortunately not to the extent that the supporters of this theory had hoped. As Milton Gordon points out in his book, *Assimilation in American Life*, policies stemming from the theory of the melting pot never got off the ground, and the government did not seriously pursue its objectives. The melting pot notion of social integration continued to persist, but only as a theory to which politicians paid lip service. The idea that American society really *is* a melting pot is another American myth that helps the established cultural elite retain its hegemonic control.

In Canada, history took a different turn. Although the Americans had liberated themselves from the yoke of British imperialism, Canadians chose to remain loyal to the British Crown. Republicanism was to be avoided at all costs — a goal that would be achieved by reinforcing ties to England. Canada's system of government, its laws, and its cultural institutions had been created to parallel, as much as conditions could permit, their British counterparts. The Canadian power elite developed and prospered within this particular cultural ideological framework. It was best not to recast political and economic systems along nationalist Canadian lines, but to retain and strengthen imperial connections. Canada's identity was to be established in reference to the "mother" country.

Another factor serving to enhance Canada's cultural links to England is our relationship with our neighbours to the south. The U.S. emerged from its revolutionary war as a strong, independent nation with sufficient political, economic, and cultural clout and ambition to pose a threat to Canada. To appreciate the seriousness of the threat to Canada, one need only look south of the Rio Grande to realize how much of the American Southwest — Texas, Colorado, Arizona, New Mexico, and California — was taken away from Mexico. It did not help Mexico that Spain had been in no shape to help its former colonies. As Porfirio Díaz remarked ironically, "Poor Mexico, so far from God and so close to the United States." Canada's concerns about U.S. "Manifest Destiny" — expansion throughout the Americas — were legitimized by a series of conflicts during the nineteenth century between the British and the Americans, including the War of 1812. It was felt Canada could pursue a separate course from the Americans only if imperial ties with England were strengthened.

Canada alone was not economically or politically capable of bridging all its differences and distances and emerging as a political and cultural entity. This political and cultural climate — at least as it was perceived by the makers of Canadian policies — would not be conducive to policies supporting the melting-pot model. A Canadian entity would not be forged by merging the colonial and immigrant populations and their varied traditions. Instead, the expectation was that immigrants should assimilate to British cultural values and swear allegiance to the British Crown.

Nonetheless, the theory of the melting pot also caught the imaginations of some Canadians. As Canadian Ralph Connor wrote in *The Foreigner* in 1904, "Out of breeds diverse in traditions, in ideals, in speech and in manner of life, Saxon and Slav, Teutonic, Celt and Gaul, one people is being made. The blood strains will mingle in the blood of a race greater than the greatest of them all."[10] Clearly, this is an iteration of the American melting-pot theory. Canadian policy-makers, however, never considered policies to support such a vision, instead concurring with the views of the Canadian elite, who saw assimilation as more conducive to their aspirations and needs.

As we have already pointed out, the assimilation model was doomed to fail, as it did not consider the inclinations of newcomers themselves or the social impact of introducing millions of immigrants. The melting-pot theory fails in the same way. It is lacking not because its objectives are unattainable, but because it does not deal with the nature of immigration, immigrants' roles in society, or the historical realities of the society they are joining. The theory revolves around an unexplained positivism without asking some fundamental questions. For example, it fails to consider the predisposition of the host society to receive immigrants. It does not consider what type of structures would be needed to amalgamate the many different cultures acting out their cultural differences in society, and it overlooks historical realities and other objective factors. It also fails to create or promote social structures that could encourage different cultures to come together. Most important, it does not consider what material and psychological incentives would be required for the immigrants to retain their cultures and to propel them into the wider, developing culture of the new country. The theory simply assumes all the different cultures will naturally come together, fuse, and give form to a new, original and vibrant culture.

Advocates of the theory of the melting pot were certainly well intentioned. They wanted a culturally harmonious society, not through assimilation — which would subjugate the immigrants — but through equal participation by all cultural groups. Its exponents were motivated by humanitarian ideals and respectful of ethnic differences. Adherents regarded the model as a step forward and away from the assimilation model favoured by the Daughters of the Empire and similar groups, who felt that "others" should become like them, though they themselves should not be touched or influenced by cultures beyond the English realm.

Unfortunately, neither the Canadian nor American governments ever formulated or put forward concrete policies to promote such a society. As American sociologist Milton Gordon comments, such objectives were never pursued. The irony was that ethnics did share their customs with others, married outside their own cultural groups, and adopted cultural traits as they saw fit. Jazz emerged from the African-American music tradition and became an American art form. Pizza and hamburgers, with their respective origins in Naples and Hamburg, became American and Canadian staples. The rodeo, originally a Mexican celebration of horse-straddling dexterity, would become a symbol of the American and Canadian West.

Observing the models of assimilation and the melting pot, we can certainly see that both have had demonstrable effects on Canadian society. We must not forget the countless immigrants and their descendants who immersed themselves in the dominant culture and who, for all intents and purposes, severed ties with their ancestral cultures. Just as important, we must recognize that a certain amount of cultural mixing has taken place. Whether it has been a result of intermarriages or of immigrants working side by side with other immigrants and with workers from the dominant culture, or simply people connecting through the business of everyday living, if there has not been a total melt, at least a little thaw has occurred. Everyone has taken and given to some degree and, consequently, Canadian culture does not have the purely English character that assimilationists strived to establish and maintain. In this ongoing discussion, and perhaps in the search by social scientists and activists for a pure and undisputable model to adhere to, it is often forgotten that both processes have occurred simultaneously in American and Canadian society.

The Policy of Multiculturalism

In this social context of partial assimilation, intermingling, and coming together of cultures, and with some enduring pockets of ethnic social behaviour, the theory of cultural pluralism began to advance. This theory provided an alternative for those who saw assimilation as distasteful and the melting pot as unhelpful. Cultural pluralism, a contemporary offshoot of philosophical relativism, actually dates to the early stages of recorded philosophical discourse. In the ancient philosophical debates in the Agora of Athens, the intellectual elite had postulated the issue of socializing divergent cultures. If civilization, as a concept, means people coming together harmoniously, then learning how to do that better will always be a primary concern of people.

In the early twentieth century, the discussion on cultural pluralism surfaced again. Unfortunately, the rise of fascism and Nazism and their brutal experiments in social engineering stopped all that. After the Second World War, cultural pluralism began to be presented again as an alternative to the theories of assimilation and the melting pot. A new world had to be established in which capital and resources were set on broader and firmer grounds, with commercial and political structures to facilitate their flow. People would need to be able to move more easily in an ever more connected world. Doors had to open again to a supply of young workers to power the growth of developing economies. Emigration–immigration and cultural pluralism would serve that.

As far back as 1915, cultural pluralism — or multiculturalism, as it was later called in Canada — was proposed as an alternative for the social integration of immigrants. American sociologist Horace Kallen, in a number of articles that appeared in the pages of *The Nation*, began to point out the impracticality of both the assimilation and melting-pot theories. Kallen reflected on the fact that immigrants were neither being assimilated by the broader society nor "melting" into it. Instead, various cultural groups were emerging and forming what he described as "a co-operation of cultural diversities, as a federation or commonwealth of national cultures."[11] As Kallen saw it, impediments to this process came from the concepts of assimilation and of the melting pot, which hampered the full cultural realization of each ethnic group. Kallen further pointed out that if ethnic groups were to be left to develop their own cultures in their new home country, each would find its own geographical, political, and cultural enclave, and the U.S. would take a form that "would be that of the federal republic; its substance a democracy of nationalities, cooperating voluntarily and autonomously through common institutions in the enterprise of self-realization through the perfection of man according to their kind."[12] It was Kallen who coined the term "cultural pluralism," although the concept itself was not properly elaborated at the time.

The new term gained ground among academics, but neither the mechanics of implementing it nor the wider effects that it would set in motion were explained. As Milton Gordon points out,

If one inquires, however, as to the specific nature
of the communication and interaction which is to
exist between the various ethnic communities and
between the individuals who compose them in
the "ideal" cultural pluralistic society, the answer
does not emerge clearly from Kallen's descrip-
tions. On the one hand, he is opposed to "ghetto"
existence and group isolation and favours creative
interaction. On the other hand, he is against the
dissolution of the communities. The nature of the
types and varieties of interaction and communication which will obviate the former alternative
and ensure the latter is a question of considerable
complexity which demands careful social and
psychological analysis.[13]

Gordon goes on to assess Kallen's theory as something that "tends
to be embodied in a general framework of rhetoric and philosophical analysis which has not pushed to the fore that kind of rigorous
sociological inquiry which the crucial importance of the idea ultimately demands."[14] Nonetheless, the theory of cultural pluralism in
Canada would win the day.

Assimilation became passé and cultural pluralism took its
place as the appropriate way to integrate newcomers into Canadian
society. In the post-war world, it was becoming increasingly evident that monocultural societies belonged to the past. Cultural
pluralism was a welcome fact of life in modern society, one to be
encouraged. Within this perspective, immigrants did not need to
be assimilated or melted into anything. Their cultures should be
socially accepted and preserved.

From the theory of cultural pluralism, the official *Canadian
Multiculturalism Act*, which we will refer to as the policy of

multiculturalism, was formed and eventually presented to Canada's Parliament as an official alternative to assimilation. That successive governments of Canada have continued to support such a dramatic shift — from Anglo-Canadians considering immigrant cultures inferior and limited, to the position that all cultures are equal and hence deserving of the opportunity for survival — is quite remarkable. We will not discuss here why there has been such a turnabout in Canadian politics, but the fact remains that it has taken place, and that this new position permits the immigrant groups to bring their culture out of their family rooms and into the public. The policy has created the possibility for immigrants to speak about their diversity and not hide it. In this sense, it is to be praised. However, this is not the entire picture.

The questionable aspect of this policy is that it reflects a notion of culture that does not correspond to the daily life experience of immigrants. The dynamic relationship between immigrants' culture and their new social role is not given any consideration. Culture is taken as something static and as an ideal to which one emotionally relates, not the dialectical result of the immigrants' cultural heritage in conjunction with their new social roles and new milieu.

If culture is, as cultural anthropologist E.B. Tylor described it, a "complex whole which includes knowledge, belief, art, morals, law, custom, and any other capabilities and habits acquired by man as a member of society,"[15] then people who had known a certain culture in their former countries would have to undergo some minor and major cultural changes, as would the culture of the new country as a result of their presence. How would, let us say, people with a peasant background and a cultural heritage suitable to that way of life be able to survive in an industrial capitalist society unless their culture went through some transformation? By failing to consider the adaptation of a particular culture to a new set of social conditions, the policy of multiculturalism reveals itself to be a liberal ideology lacking sociological considerations. Certainly, culture cannot be pickled like a vegetable to retain its consistency and freshness! Nevertheless, in October 1971, a year after the October Crisis had prompted Prime Minister Trudeau to invoke the *War Measures Act*, he proposed to the House of Commons the policy of multiculturalism, which would help ethnic groups "preserve their culture." The policy was immediately passed. It was presented as the tangible proof of Canada's tolerant nature, and it became an object of national pride: Canada was unlike the U.S. melting pot; Canada was able to formulate its own social theory vis-à-vis ethnicity; and Canada had the courage to implement programs reflecting the nature of such a theory. Unfortunately, it did not quite live up to such billing. The formulation of the theory was nothing new. The implementation of such a policy was also nothing new or unique. We should be aware that Australia was simultaneously pursuing a similar multicultural policy, and that in many parts of the U.S., policies promoting cultural pluralism have been in place since before 1971. As Howard Brotz pointed out in the journal *Canadian Public Policy*, "The greatest disservice that has been done to a correct self-understanding of Canadian society has been the invention of the fiction that the United States and Canada differ in their ethnic relations on grounds of 'principle.'"[16] In South Africa, cultural pluralism is the policy of the government, but it is also enshrined in law. Each ethnic group is forced to practise its social and racial diversity. In other words, Canadian pride in the novelty, originality, and unique nature of its policy is exaggerated.

Social Conditions Pre-Dating the Policy of Multiculturalism

Before we describe and analyze the policy objectives of multiculturalism, let us take a bird's-eye view of the Canadian social conditions of the early 1960s as they related to immigrants, Canadian ethnic minorities, and their cultural and social aspirations. We want to look at how the significant flow of immigrants affected Canadian society, and how those immigrants integrated with the fabric of their new society.

Immigration has had a tremendous effect on Canadian life. Whether it has been the large influx of Irish immigrants in the nineteenth century, or of Eastern and Southern Europeans in the twentieth century, or the subsequent waves of immigration from the Third World, it is fair to say immigrants have contributed immeasurably to Canada's economic development.

Beyond economic development, these waves of large-scale immigration also brought about changes in the social fabric of the nation. An 1871 government Census revealed that slightly more than 60 percent of Canada's population was of British origin, and 31 percent was French. This shows that only 9 percent of Canada's population was not of these two origins. A little more than a century later, the composition of Canada's population had changed dramatically. A 1981 Census showed that the proportion of the population from British backgrounds had fallen to 44 percent, while the proportion from French backgrounds remained about the same. By then, people who were neither British nor French had come to represent nearly a quarter of the population.

Not only did immigration bring demographic changes in relation to ancestral background, but it also gave rise to a large network of ethnicity-based socio-cultural organizations. The development of the ethnic media from the early twentieth century through to the 1960s illustrates this phenomenon well. A study prepared for the Royal Commission of Bilingualism and Biculturalism in 1965–66 notes the growth of the ethnic press:

> There were two Slavic publications in 1905, but
> in 1965 there were fifty-four, thirty-three of them

Ukrainian. The Roman languages groups had only two Italian publications in 1911; by 1965 they had a total of fourteen: eleven Italian and three Portuguese. Before the First World War, the publications of the German groups outnumbered those of the Slavic group by twelve to one and most of them were in German language. The Scandinavian groups also had a few periodicals. The Dutch ethnic press did not appear until the 1950s, when a dozen periodicals were founded. Publication in languages that did not fall within the main groups of German, Slavic or Romanic languages have grown shown a variable rate of growth, although taken together they rose from eight in 1911 to 57 in 1965.[17]

Those huge increases in the publications of the ethnic press reflected the needs of a large portion of the Canadian population who demanded more than the English and French publications were providing.

The same phenomenon has occurred with most of the other social, cultural, and economic institutions of the nation. Ethnic populations who were not served by or satisfied with existing institutions established their own. Ethnic businesses, set up to cater to the needs and tastes of ethnic populations, have developed immensely, especially since the Second World War. Ethnic social agencies have been established to deal with specific problems facing newcomers arriving from particular places, and cultural organizations have emerged to provide immigrants with a sense of cultural continuity and security. Hence, not only has Canada's population become more ethnically heterogeneous, but a structural growth of the ethnic communities has also taken place.

Immigrant communities have grown not just demographically but also in terms of wealth. A corresponding social stratification has occurred, featuring an actual middle class with its own set of social and economic needs. This development is significant because it has emerged from ethnic groups' inherited cultures while it is also consonant with their new society. Such an independent and parallel evolution, as we shall see later, is also reflected in the newcomers' ever-changing informal spoken language.

Undoubtedly, immigrants to Canada were sought largely to fill out low-level occupational ranks. As celebrated Canadian sociologist John Porter notes in his influential text, *The Vertical Mosaic*, "Most of Canada's minority groups have at some time had this entrance status."[18] However, Porter also points out that some have been able to move past the starting gate into a more diverse range of occupations. Businessmen, professionals, and skilled workers have emerged from the ranks of newcomers, often by serving their own communities, reaching higher social and economic status within those communities.

As these structural changes and developments have taken place, Canadian society has remained culturally closed and unreceptive to the immigrants' needs and aspirations. A new policy would be needed to reflect the changing social conditions and go beyond the static cultural and social climate that had remained virtually unaltered since the beginning of immigration. By the mid-1960s, it was becoming painfully apparent that a government with democratic institutions and of a democratic tradition needed to respond to the needs and wants of a changed nation, and the Liberal government ultimately set up its Royal Commission on Bilingualism and Biculturalism.

Chapter 2

The Royal Commission and the Resulting Policy of Multiculturalism

Amid vast democratic changes in Canada, the structural growth of ethnic communities, the dynamic social development within ethnic communities, open discrimination against many immigrants, and immigrants' refusal to submit to cultural extinction, the RCBB was established. In 1963, Prime Minister Lester Pearson appointed the Commission to "inquire into and report upon the existing state of bilingualism and biculturalism in Canada" and "recommend what steps should be taken to develop the Canadian Confederation on the basis of an equal partnership between the two founding races, taking into account the contributions made by the other ethnic groups to the cultural enrichment of Canada and the measures that should be taken to safeguard that contribution."[1]

Essentially, the Commission was mandated to explore the cultural forces at work in Canadian society, to give positive shape to their expression, and to make the appropriate recommendations to the government. After a lengthy enquiry, most of the recommendations the Commission made were accepted and reflected in the subsequent policy of multiculturalism. The recommendations of the RCBB to the government fell largely within four categories: human rights, language rights, the media, and cultural assistance. However, as we shall see, a number of the recommendations were deferred or not considered at all.

In their first set of recommendations, the commissioners asked the federal and provincial governments to enact laws that would make illegal any discrimination based on race, creed, colour, nationality, ancestry, or place of origin. In the second set, dealing with language rights, the commissioners recommended that the federal government have a language policy to provide special instruction in the appropriate official language "for children who enter the public school system with an inadequate knowledge of that language."[2] It also recommended that children have the opportunity to learn languages other than English and French through the public school system.

The third set of recommendations, dealing with the media, suggested that the Canadian Radio and Television Commission "remove restrictions on private broadcasting in languages other than English and French"[3] and that the Canadian Radio-television and Telecommunications Commission (CRTC) "undertake studies in the field of broadcasting in other languages to determine the best means by which radio and television can contribute to the maintenance of languages and cultures."[4] It also recommended that the Canadian Broadcasting Corporation (CBC) recognize the place of other languages in its programs and that the National Film Board continue to develop films that informed Canadians about one another.

In their fourth category of recommendations, dealing with the question of ethnic cultural retention, the commissioners pointed to the need to help ethnocultural groups financially through federal, provincial, and municipal agencies. The government needed to fund and research "organizations whose objectives are to foster the arts and letters of cultural groups other than the British and French," their report said.[5]

The RCBB made its final report to the government on October 23, 1969. Two years later, the Liberal government submitted a document to Parliament for approval. It laid out the government's response to the Commission's recommendations and presented the policy of multiculturalism. Although most recommendations received highly favourable responses, some were either rejected or consigned to the nebulous area of "further studies."

The recommendations dealing with human rights and the encouragement for ethnic groups to preserve their cultures were readily accepted. In relation to the former, as *Hansard* recorded, the government stated that the *Canadian Election Act* (proclaimed April 12, 1971) and upcoming amendments to the *Citizenship Act* dealt with the human rights recommendations and insofar as these recommendations related to the provincial laws, the federal government responded that it had the whole question of human rights under consideration.

Similarly, in the case where funding was recommended for an organization that would foster the cultural activities of a group other than the British and French, the government responded directly that grants programs would provide funds to assist such organizations.

The recommendations dealing with the media and the education of ethnic children, however, met with a decidedly mixed response. On one hand, the CRTC agreed to place the matter of restrictions on private broadcasting in languages other than English in the hands of the Commission, paving the way for the removal of those restrictions. On the other hand, the CBC did not agree with the spirit of the recommendation to broadcast programs in languages other than English and French.

Similarly, the Commission's recommendations that the teaching of languages other than English and French be incorporated as options in public elementary school programs were deferred to the provincial governments. The federal government promised to study the relationship between language and cultural retention and supported the recommendation to provide instruction in the appropriate official language to children who did not speak that language. Although both dealt with education, a jurisdictional responsibility of provincial governments, the federal government lent its support to only one of the recommendations, choosing not to deal with the more controversial issue of third-language instruction, seeing it as having potential for political conflict.

Undoubtedly, the spirit contained in Book IV of the RCBB was retained in the federal government's response to the recommendations, although, as we have seen, not all the Commission's recommendations met its approval.

Ultimately, though, what is more important to this analysis is not what was omitted or included in the policy compared with the recommendations, but differences in the terms of reference and in the assumptions made by the commissioners versus those made by the policy-makers of multiculturalism. The commissioners had taken pains to establish complete and accurate terms of reference, specifically clarifying what they meant by founding nations, ethnic groups, and culture. In framing the policy of multiculturalism, the government changed the terms of reference and assumptions that flowed from them, permitting a different vision of what Canadian society was, or ought to be. Consequently, the new policy permitted social groups to view it as an instrument for realizing particularistic visions of Canadian society regarding ethnic groups. These differing assumptions form the basis for different, sometimes problematic, interpretations of the policy of multiculturalism. In turn, as we shall see, the debatable validity of these interpretations hinges on the correctness of the assumptions.

From the outset of their process, the commissioners had recognized the significant impact that their terms of reference and their definitions could have on the entire proceedings and on the eventual recommendations they would make to the government. In the introduction to their report, they stated that the definitions of the terms of reference "often imply the adoption of a point of view."[6] They took care to recognize that a point of view — which we may call a vision or ideology — could ultimately shape the direction of their findings and recommendations, which could in turn shape the policy of multiculturalism and the ways it was to be interpreted.

The commissioners took the view that Canadian society had been shaped by two founding peoples: the French and the English. To them this did not mean "a kind of hereditary aristocracy composed of two founding peoples, perpetuating itself from father to son, and a lower order of other ethnic groups, forever excluded from spheres of influence."[7] Instead, it was an acknowledgement, as they wrote, of the "undisputed role played by Canadians of French and British origin in 1867, and long before Confederation"[8] in the structuring of the political and social system of Canada. This was merely their acknowledgement of an historical fact.

The other term the commissioners found necessary to define was "ethnic groups." For them, belonging to an ethnic group is a subjective issue and is not determined merely by "the statistical category covering those having a certain ethnic origin."[9] Being ethnic, in their determination, was based on one's "feeling of belonging to the group." The commissioners also made a connection between ethnicity and immigration, pointing to two things: that ethnics are those who have come to Canada with an origin other than French or British, and that the term does not apply to the Indigenous population. The term "ethnic groups" for them meant "those peoples of diverse origin who come to Canada during or after the founding of the Canadian state and that it does not include the first inhabitants of this country."[10]

The commissioners also found it pertinent that culture was by necessity connected to language. "Culture," as they indicated, "and the language that serves as its vehicle cannot be dissociated. Language allows for self-expression and communication according to one's own logic."[11] The commissioners intended these definitions to serve as the foundation for policies regarding social and cultural issues.

In the policy of multiculturalism, these assumptions either differ significantly or are missing entirely. The policy makes no reference to the historical fact that Canada, as the nation state we know today, was founded by two original groups, the French and the English, even though this historical reality was the essential context in which subsequent immigration took place and the reason why ethnic groups came into existence.

Furthermore, contrary to the statement of the Commission that the term "ethnic" referred to anyone who was not of French, British, or Native origin, the official policy of multiculturalism assumes that all Canadians, including these groups, are ethnics. Taking this position diminished the complex historical dynamics that had developed between the charter groups, Native peoples, and the immigrant population as they shaped a new society. It is interesting to note that Prime Minister Trudeau agreed with the commissioners that one's ethnicity was a subjective choice, recognizing that "the individual's freedom would be hampered if he were locked for life within a particular cultural compartment by the accident of birth or language."[12] However, stating at the same time that "we are all ethnics" in effect forces an individual to choose an ethnic group to which he or she should belong. Another major difference between the commissioners' terms of reference and those of the resulting policy of multiculturalism relates to the question of culture. The commissioners had taken pains to define culture and point out that it was intrinsically linked to language. Trudeau contradicted this by stating that "although there are two official languages, there is no official culture."[13]

The point here is not merely to catalogue the similarities and differences between the recommendations of the RCBB and the policy of multiculturalism. It is to point out that a shift had occurred — one that could permit a different vision of Canadian society. The commissioners' assumptions defined a Canadian society structured by two founding groups, French and English, with Native populations recognized as distinct, but not as "ethnics" — as later arrivals of immigrants would be. In this order of things, ethnic groups had developed within a society where the legal, political, and socio-economic systems had already established a particular character. It is important that this is recognized so that the actions of ethnic activists can be of substance.

The shifts that have occurred in the policy of multiculturalism have hidden this reality and have left us with uncertain reference points to use as a basis for social and political action. For example, when the policy stated there was "no official Canadian culture," it implied that Canadian culture was composed of the separate activities of all ethnocultural groups, and that no difference existed between the contributions or influence of Indigenous peoples, the charter groups, and the later waves of immigrants. In the same breath, the policy stated there were only two official languages: English and French. If we believe, as we do, that culture and language cannot be separated and are functions of one another, then one statement negates the other. While the first essentially promotes the view of Canada as an ethnocultural mosaic in which all cultures have equal rights, the latter recognizes that a difference exists between the two charter groups and the ethnic ones that emerged as a result of immigration.

It is this lack of clear perspective that prompted Monique Bégin to state, in a 1976 speech at the Second Conference of Multiculturalism, "The objectives of multiculturalism in relation to national unity, and to the integration to active Canadian life of immigrants and new Canadians, have never been clearly stated.

Nor has the fine line between multiculturalism and multilingualism been drawn. I think the distinction between multiculturalism and immigration has never been made, either."[14] Professor Howard Brotz of McMaster University also points out the ambiguity of this policy. According to him, the ambiguity is deliberate, reflecting the immigrants' integration into Canadian society. He goes on to point out that this is also a by-product of Trudeau's attempt to deal with growing unrest in Quebec.[15]

Critics who attack the policy for its lack of clarity often miss the mark. They tend to focus on its objective rather than its lack of a clear vision. The objective itself is fairly clear: to give assistance to all those ethnic groups who want to preserve and develop their cultural identities. The "muddle" stems from the absence of a vision, and also from the lack of definition of what is an ethnic group and what is or could be its culture. Further, it does not provide a sense of direction of how the ethnic groups and their cultures can become part of wider Canadian society.

This lack of clear harbingers in the policy has led to different views of what Canadian society is, what it should or could be, and what the policy of multiculturalism should and could do. The policy has allowed different social forces — ethnic and otherwise — to develop different perspectives on the question of ethnic groups and their social presence in Canadian society. Undoubtedly, the policy of multiculturalism has given us a base from which we can choose a number of political and social programs, but its assumptions about what constitutes Canadian society are not clear. It brings to mind Italian dramatist Luigi Pirandello's *Six Characters in Search of an Author*, where six characters live a nebulous existence because they lack an author to give them concreteness. In our case, the lack of a clear vision of the fundamentals of Canadian culture leads to a desperate search for a vision of Canadian society that could be used as a reference point.

Our task at this point becomes to synthesize these different points of view, analyzing their assumptions and determining their ideological orientation. Although this approach runs the risk of simplifying views that at times are complex and deserve more than specific labels attached to them, it nonetheless enables us to understand what was sought by and what could be asked of the policy of multiculturalism, and what type of Canadian society was envisioned in terms of its ethnic components.

Differing Approaches to the Policy of Multiculturalism

On the whole, it is safe to state that the demands made by ethnic groups, politicians, educators, and social scientists can be seen from three different perspectives, each looking at the policy of multiculturalism from its own vantage point and bending it as suitable. These three perspectives can be categorized as follows: multiculturalism as tokenism, the mosaic concept of multiculturalism, and multiculturalism as a sharing and merging of different cultural traditions. Let us examine separately these three perspectives, beginning with the tokenistic nature of the policy.

As has been stated, the policy of multiculturalism was incidental. That is to say, it stemmed from a political action to curb the demands of French-Canadians, especially separatists, to recognize and protect their language and culture. In a sense, creating the policy was a stroke of political genius on the part of the Trudeau government to defuse the tense political situation in Quebec and at the same time appease some demands made by ethnic populations. As such, the programs that emerged from the policy were tokenistic — not much more than support for some ethnic songs and dances. The picture that emerged was one of a Canadian society with an already established cultural tradition moving forward with its pre-existing cultural and social institutions intact. Any celebration of ethnic diversity in such a case would be relegated to Canada's social periphery, where it would add a bit of colour and spice, but not much more. The statement of the policy itself clearly pointed out that ethnic cultural expression would be taking place within a bilingual framework. This in essence removed the necessary linkage of language and culture, and as the commissioners had stated explicitly, it would only lead to patronizing, superficial expressions of ethnic cultures.

That this was the preferred course of action for the established social, cultural, and political forces should not be surprising. It provided a release of pent-up energy through a flurry of activities without making any meaningful changes. It would take only a few million dollars to allow ethnic groups to celebrate their cultural heritage. Kogila Moodley points to the harmless and insubstantial nature of this implementation of the policy of multiculturalism: "As long as cultural persistence is confined to food, clothes, dance, and music, then cultural diversity provides colour to an otherwise mundane monotonous technological society."[16] As such, it would pose no threat and, worse, would trivialize, neutralize, and absorb social and economic inequalities. Ethnicity displayed and acted out in this manner would be apparent, but harmless.

That the advantaged groups, or the Canadian elite, would prefer this course should be obvious. What perhaps is more surprising was the favourable response of "ethnic leaders" to this interpretation of the policy. To those accustomed to an assimilationist mentality and to the expectation to conform, the policy appeared to be a blessing. It would legitimize their ethnic differences and permit ethnic groups to bring them into the open, while appearing to give them economic and socio-political power in the process.

The acceptance of the policy in this form was also facilitated by a reluctance to rethink Canadian society in a way that would accommodate the social needs of its ethnic populations. The only demands on the existing establishment would revolve around a superficial and tokenistic recognition of their folkloric past. It was Monique Bégin again who questioned this form of multiculturalism, pointing to the questionable interests of ethnic leaders who welcomed it: "Poor folklore dances, lousy handicrafts, local newspapers with nothing on Canada, or little clannish egocentric group meetings are not multicultural, in my way of thinking. In fact, I should go so far as saying they do a disservice to the 17 and some million dollars already devoted to the program from the beginning to the end of 1976."[17] She went on to say that this type of multiculturalism was of "no interest and of no value to Canadians, since it only serves the personal interest of small establishments, if I may say, using multiculturalism as a selfish channel for their own promotion."[18] That these types of programs would soon fail to satisfy the ethnic population was not difficult to foresee.

Ethnic cultural activists began to understand that they could — and should — be drawing more from their pool of cultural resources than folkloric songs and dances. As they became more aware of their substantial contributions to Canadian society, they began to demand their presence be more substantially represented in the established institutions of the land. Furthermore, to gain or build credibility and respect in their own communities, their spokespeople have recognized they needed to address issues such as racism, exclusion from influential positions, low income, and myriad other problems that ethnic communities faced in establishing themselves firmly in Canadian society.

Multiculturalism — a policy openly calling for the advancement of ethnic groups within the framework of the larger Canadian society — could not stand as a mere nod to ethnic citizens' cultural past. The demands of ethnic groups, conscious of their contributions to the general development of Canadian society, had to be recognized in concrete, substantial, and lasting ways. In the pale light of multicultural tokenism, some social scientists and ethnic leaders began to drift toward the model of the mosaic.

Needless to say, the progression from the tokenistic form of multiculturalism to a more substantial one that aspires to represent actual and current cultural experiences and the true social and economic needs of newcomers has not been linear. In fact, many ethnic organizations are still content to project their images only through costumes and festivals and to limit their aspirations to writing applications to fund their annual banquets or picnics. However, what has to be said here is that multiculturalism in the form of mere tokenism is not the ultimate ethnic aspiration.

In fact, multiculturalism that disregards the commissioners' forewarning would not be in the interest of ethnic communities. The concept of the mosaic has commanded the attention of some scholars, earned the fervent support of many ethnic activists and, to some extent, has even become fashionable. It has become an ideology, and as such demands to be analyzed. We, as ethnic activists, need to do that. We need to formulate a position in support of or in opposition to the mosaic view of Canadian society. If we find it wanting, we must provide a better vision for integrating newcomers than the tokenistic interpretation of the policy of multiculturalism and the ideology of the mosaic. For now, let us look at the vision of the mosaic and determine its viability.

The essential position of the holders of the mosaic view is that Canadian society is composed of many different enclaves, each representing a particular ethnic culture. The role of ethnic activists in this model is to make each piece of the mosaic equal in importance, status, and power. We must evaluate this vision and determine the validity of its assumptions. We also need to look at the political and economic forces that support it, including who will be the winners and losers if the vision comes to fruition. A substantial analysis of this vision is necessary, in our view, as the idea of the mosaic has captured the attention of so many ethnic and non-ethnic social activists and has become an ideological reference point for resolving the ethnic question. Whether it is in relation to the current struggle at the Toronto Board of Education over heritage language classes, petitions to the CRTC for more ethnic broadcasting, or lobbying efforts for greater funding for ethnic cultural activities, the notion that Canada is an ethnic mosaic is constantly evoked. We need to scrutinize this ideological position, because we fear that orienting the struggle of the ethnic groups from this perspective could lead to a cul-de-sac that leaves Canada's ethnic communities without tangible advances, frustrated, embittered, and resentful of each other and of Canadian society.

Chapter 3

The Ideology of the Mosaic

The view that Canada is a mosaic composed of many ethnocultural groups predates, by many years, the policy of multiculturalism introduced by Parliament. In fact, as with many other things, it came to us from our southern neighbours. It was 1922 when an American, Victoria Hayward, introduced the concept in a book titled *Romantic Canada*. The concept was further elaborated by Kate A. Foster in 1926, in *Our Canadian Mosaic*, and by S.D. Clark in a series of articles in the 1950s. Finally, Canadian author John Porter further expanded on it in 1965, lending it unquestionable sociological legitimacy.

As a result, since then most sociologists have assumed that Canadian society has not been able to assimilate its different ethnic groups, and neither did Canada "melt down" the ethnics to fashion a new society. The popular academic notion, instead, is that ethnocultural groups have flourished independently throughout the years, each within its own enclave of Canadian society. According to this view, Canada is a pluralistic society, partly as a result of the massive technological and industrial developments of the twentieth century, but mainly because of its regional and cultural differences. At the root of this diversity is ethnicity. The cultural life of Canada, it is believed, is the sum of all its ethnocultures, not in aggregated form, but in distinct parts. The assumption affirms that what keeps the members of these ethnic groups together, and what keeps each ethnic group apart from the others, is a distinction based on primordial feelings. This separation can be witnessed culturally, socially, and geographically in terms of the territory each ethnic group occupies. In this way, we cannot speak of Canadians, or of a Canadian culture, without adding another national adjective. We all become hyphenated Canadians: Greco-Canadians, Italian-Canadians, Indo-Canadians, and so on. The metaphor of the mosaic appropriately describes this view of Canadian society.

Sociologist Leo Driedger, in *The Canadian Ethnic Mosaic*, fully subscribes to this view, dividing Canada into six major regions, giving each a particular ethnic character.

The Northlands comprises the Yukon, the Northwest Territories, and the northern parts of British Columbia, Alberta, Saskatchewan, Manitoba, Ontario, and Quebec. This is the region of Native peoples, and its multilingualism and multiculturalism derive from its various "ethnic" Native groups, and some European groups who settled there.

The West includes the southern portions of British Columbia, Alberta, Saskatchewan, and Manitoba, in which four major ethnic groups are found: British, German, Ukrainian, and French, plus a number of smaller ones.

Upper Canada is southern Ontario, with its dominant British "ethnic" group intermingled with other ethnic groups from northern and southern Europe and the Third World.

Driedger describes Lower Canada as the region of southern Quebec, which is exclusively French-Canadian.

Moving east, he describes the Maritimes (Newfoundland, Nova Scotia, Prince Edward Island) as unilingual, and unicultural because 95 percent speak English at home.

Finally, there is New Brunswick, which is bilingual and bicultural, where one-fourth of the people speak French at home, while the rest speak English.

This, according to Driedger is the regional ethnic mosaic.[1]

Pure nonsense!

John Porter, in *The Vertical Mosaic*, introduces another factor that divides Canada's ethnic populations: social status. His view is that the "Anglo ethnic group" is dominant and occupies the higher spheres of political and economic control. In this social dynamic, the "other" ethnic groups, including French-Canadians, play subservient roles. Because of this, he says, not only do we have an ethnocultural mosaic in Canada, but also a hierarchy in which the "other" ethnic groups occupy the lower rungs of society.[2]

In essence, this is what is meant when we refer to Canada as a mosaic. The metaphor conjures images of distinct ethnocultural groups spatially segregated and operating within their own social structures. But the metaphor of the mosaic is not just a model for describing our ethnic social formations. It is also a vision of what Canadian society should be. It becomes, in fact, a motivating force to shape Canadian society along this line. It is an ideology that interprets social events and attempts to align them with its vision.

An ideology, in our minds, consists of two essential elements. First, it is a vision that adopts a particular interpretation of social events. Second, it is an intellectual motive force that not only interprets social events, but also tries to direct political and social action in keeping with its vision. The view of Canadian society as an ethnic mosaic features these two defining aspects of ideology. The people and forces that maintain this view try to interpret Canadian society from an ethnic perspective. We have just discussed two examples in which regional differences and income status are explained through ethnicity at the expense of other social and historical factors. The demands these forces make of society focus on the welfare of ethnic groups and try to channel their social and intellectual energies from an ethnocentric perspective. In this sense, we can say that labelling Canadian society as a mosaic is not just a metaphorical way of describing it. It is ideological. It interprets social events and directs their outcomes to suit its objectives.

The Relationship Between Assumption and Ideology

Before we move to an analysis of the specific demands made by proponents of the ideology of the mosaic or of the policies that can result from such an ideology, it is necessary to look at the assumptions that form its foundation. An awareness and analysis of these assumptions should reveal the nature of the ideology and its validity. What determines the social validity of an ideology is not, in our opinion, the objective it aims to achieve but the correctness of its assumptions when compared to a particular social reality. Let us explain.

Our assumptions lead us to make choices in social situations. Although the starting point is the same and the final outcome may be similar, the ideologies that inform how people or groups approach a situation can be completely different.

For example, if we acknowledge the existence of poverty in Canada and we all want to eliminate it, a different number of possible solutions could emerge. This is so because of the different ideologies we could apply to the question, which depend on the assumptions we make about a problem. It might be assumed that people are poor because they are lazy, or that flaws in the market system do not permit a fair distribution of goods, or that the poor are poor because they have been exploited by others. These three different assumptions may lead to three different ideological approaches to the same question. A policy related to the first assumption — laziness — might propose to motivate people to take more action to help themselves. Those behind the second assumption might suggest restructuring the system so the market can function more smoothly and efficiently. The third may propose ways to end exploitation.

In these hypothetical cases, three different assumptions drive different ideological motivations that will, in turn, generate different policies and social programs to deal with the problem. The conservative, the liberal, and the socialist may all want to resolve the problem of poverty, but each will have a different solution. Hence, a conservative might set up programs to motivate the lazy person by using a system of penalties and rewards; the liberal might try to set up a better functioning market for the distribution of wealth; and the socialist might propose ways to remove from power the class of people doing the exploitation.

The validity of a particular policy for social change is derived not from its objectives, but from the assumptions that constitute its ideological framework.

If we were to continue with our example, we would find that policies seeking to eliminate poverty through punishments and rewards would be effective only if the assumption that poverty and wealth were indeed the result of one's willingness to work. The liberal policies would have positive results only if poverty indeed were caused by malfunctions of the market system. The policies of the socialists would be effective only if, in fact, a class of people were exploiting the poor.

When a policy is implemented, the ideology behind it is put to the test. If the ideology is correct, the policies stemming from it will produce the desired results. If not, the results will differ from the goal, exposing a disjunction between the ideology and its practical implementations. Christopher Columbus's vision that navigating westward would lead him to India, based on the assumption that the world was round, was proven correct. He did not reach India, of course, but the assumption of a round world was indeed proven correct. If, on the contrary, the world was not round, instead of meeting a continent, he would have met an abyss. His vision would not have corresponded to reality and he would not have lived to tell the tale.

Let's look at the assumptions behind the ideology of the mosaic and see how they compare to reality.

For the internal logic of any ideological outlook to stand up, the assumptions it makes must not be self-contradictory. Instead, they should reinforce one another to present a unified view, with few or no internal discrepancies. In the ideology of the mosaic, such internal logic does exist. It offers a set of correlated assumptions and corollaries that present a unified logical position. Of course, we know that a perspective or an argument can be logical and still be totally incorrect. The following paragraphs deal with the assumptions made by the ideologists of the mosaic and the degree to which they correspond to reality.

We have pointed out previously that any analysis of the validity of an ideology begins by looking at the assumptions that provide its foundations. Later, it is helpful to study the results of the policies flowing from such an ideology. The first verification implies a process that compares the assumptions with the history, social conditions, and political structures of the society in question. If the policies and demands originate from a valid ideological position, their realization is possible, even if they meet considerable resistance and obstacles. If, however, they are incorrect, they can only lead to bitterness and frustration among those making the demands, and possibly to conflict with other social groups. Let us make, for the time being, an analysis of the assumptions of the ideology of the mosaic. We will return to look at its practice when we look at specific demands made by the groups who share this vision of Canadian society.

Three fundamental assumptions of the theory of the mosaic are that all Canadians are immigrants, that we are all ethnics, and that the nature of culture is primordial and unchangeable. Accepting these assumptions leads to a denial of a Canadian mainstream social group. In other words, a Canadian without another added adjective does not exist. So we would have Anglo-Canadians, French-Canadians, Ukrainian-Canadians, etc., but no one would simply be Canadian. Another central assumption held firmly by ideologists of the mosaic revolves around the question of culture. In this model, culture is viewed as unchanging and related to the primordial nature of a people. The assumptions that we are all immigrants, that we are all ethnics, and that culture is primordial and unchanging are the foundations of the ideology of the mosaic. We will see that these assumptions do not correspond to Canadian social reality and could lead to policies and programs unhelpful to the integration of newcomers. At best they will be of no consequence.

Chapter 4

The Assumption
of Immigration

We have already discussed some aspects of immigration and how the large influx of immigrants has led various Canadian governments to enact laws and policies to integrate new arrivals. We want to pick up the topic of immigration here to compare the differences it has made with other ways of populating the vast expanses of Canada, and to focus on what constitutes immigration. Theorists of the mosaic assume all Canadians are immigrants or descendants of such. We want to challenge this assertion in view of the historical processes that unfolded in populating Canada.

We know from history that large movements of people from one country to another, or one continent to another, are not events limited to either time or place. To be certain, migration has been an integral part of man's social development. People either collectively or individually have moved, for different reasons, to improve their economic and social status. Some large movements of people have been propelled by state intervention: a state would coordinate the movements of people to achieve specific objectives. For example, the invasion of the Roman Empire was a migratory movement of people pushing themselves onto Roman-administered lands. It was a common effort between leaders and their subjects to find suitable lands for settlement. Similarly, the conquest of America by Europeans and their settlement on the new continent was state directed and advantageous to the states concerned. European countries needed to populate the new continent with their own people to establish permanency and to ensure an advantageous and continuous exchange of goods. The colonizers acted under precise directives from their European states and established colonies reflecting the needs and aspirations of their respective countries.

However, the mass movement of people we refer to as emigration–immigration has a different character. Like other forms of migration, it involves great numbers of people, but it is made up of individuals and families acting independently, not pushed by particular political or military action. Their movement is not an operation directly orchestrated by the state, although states would regulate and influence such movement. Essentially, it is a migration of citizens "free" to relocate their residence and possibly adopt a new citizenship. It was mainly in the nineteenth and twentieth centuries that this form of mass movements of people began to take place. The social rank of these people, the reasons that motivated or induced them to migrate, the considerations that have pushed many nations to implement emigration or immigration policies, and the roles that governments have played in these movements are unique. Although this form of migration has occurred throughout recorded history, it has never taken place in the proportions we have seen in the last two centuries. Further, it has never been so integral to the formation and development of the socio-economic system that has prevailed in the Western world since the time of the Industrial Revolution.

If, in the past, scholars moved from Athens to Rome, or masons from Scotland to England, or rural Catalans to urban Madrid, such shifts of people from one area to another, although not socially insignificant, did not change fundamental social structures. With the Industrial Revolution, the situation changed, and the migration of individuals assumed a mass character. Since then, millions have lost their traditional livelihoods and, forced by economic necessity, transferred themselves to centres of industrial production. Independent carpenters, shoemakers, and blacksmiths have been forced to abandon their trades and villages. The market for their goods and craftsmanship was taken over by cheaper, mass-produced products from areas of industrial concentration: the factories of the cities. Human migration from country to city began in large numbers, meeting the needs of a system geared to the concentration and centralization of production, and people moved to sell their labour to the highest bidder, who needed to keep the new centres of production running and growing.

Ironically, a great number of people who fled rural areas to find employment elsewhere continued to be jobless in these new areas of population growth. New jobs in cities were all too often inadequate to support people who had come seeking better opportunities. Such developments began to give cities characteristics that are familiar to us today: massive scale and stark stratification, including slums, and crime. Cities became tense with social unrest as large reserves of unemployed people agitated for something better.

The same phenomenon began to take shape in the cities of the New World, but with distinctions that reflected their own realities. The new centres of production in the Americas did not have populated hinterlands to supply the manpower needed in urban industries, especially as the hinterlands also needed more people to extract or grow the raw materials to feed urban industries. Further, more population growth throughout the new continent was necessary to increase the domestic market for produced goods. Immigration–emigration seemed to offer a ready solution. It would accomplish two objectives: permitting European industrialists to accelerate growth without having to worry much about the social and political consequences for those left without jobs while allowing American industrialists to pursue production growth as they saw fit. Before we move to analyze what all this meant for Canada, let us consider some other ways that emigration–immigration may enhance our understanding of this phenomenon.

The massive movement of people between countries in the nineteenth and twentieth centuries was a product of the Industrial Revolution. It began to occur in the areas that had developed industries earliest. The factories first brought under their influence those people living in the vicinity of the new centres of production. As they displaced tradespeople and labourers alike, unemployment grew in Europe's industrial centres, driving people to emigrate to the New World in search of better opportunities. These were the English who came to Canada, not as the settlers or colonizers of earlier times, but as workers to fill the demands of the expanding new industries. They were the Germans who emigrated to the U.S., contributed to the growth of the union movement, and formed socialist clubs in many American cities. They were the northern Italians who emigrated to what was then called the Argentine and to many parts of the U.S., advancing trade union movements and establishing working-class parties. Over time, emigration from these areas slowed to a trickle. Immigrants were no longer predominantly English, German, or northern Italian. Instead, they were the Irish, southern Italians, other southern Europeans, and eastern Europeans as the exodus shifted from the most industrialized European centres to the least industrialized ones.

This shift is indicative of a new relationship between regions of the same country, and between countries themselves. Industrialization brought a new economic order in which stronger and more industrialized regions and nations had supremacy over less industrialized counterparts. Emigration–immigration became part of the process and people became resources to be extracted from less developed parts of the world. The local populations around the world's new and quickly growing industrial centres have never been enough to satisfy the demand for workers. Governments of industrialized countries have had to reach ever farther into the corners of the globe to source the labour they needed. Emigration–immigration was essential to this type of development: two sides of the same coin, affecting migrants' home countries and destination countries alike, answering the basic need of receiving countries to build their labour supplies and the need of sending countries to let go of their labour surpluses. Still, it was not simply a question of supply and demand, in which an oversupply of labour in one country spilled over to fill a lack of it in another. Emigration–immigration can also be a political solution that governments adopt to meet the practical demands of specific times and conditions. Emigration can be used, for example, as a safety valve to defuse potential unrest among large numbers of unemployed people. They leave the country helping to relieve the issue and the system continues without any structural change.

We have tried to explain that migration takes different forms and that there is a substantial difference between emigration–immigration and other forms of mass movements of people. Knowing the varied forces driving migration helps us understand how Canada came to be populated. This in turn can help us to understand the social dynamics that evolved between Canada's ethnic groups and what it would take to change them.

Assumptions About Immigration to Canada

The assertion that Canadians are all immigrants with the exception of the Native people is often repeated by politicians, effectively promoting the theory of the mosaic. This kind of simplistic statement, unfortunately, is uttered not just by politicians who need digestible messages to appeal to voters. Some academics have also come to accept this gross generalization, permitting them to work from an incorrect view of immigration and how Canada came to be populated. For example, John W. Berry, Rudolf Kalin, and Donald Taylor of Queen's University, in their book *Multiculturalism and Ethnic Attitudes in Canada*, start from the perspective that everyone in Canada is an immigrant, including Native peoples. They point out that people began to arrive in Canada in three phases: first, the wave of Indigenous people, followed by the wave of the British and French, then by a third wave from elsewhere in Europe and the other continents. Although such statements may seem at first glance correct, a more thorough analysis reveals their superficiality and exposes how the times and circumstances of these migrations are sharply distinct from one another, each with fundamentally different and markedly social implications for members of these groups and for Canada itself.[1]

Emigration–immigration is only one form of transnational movement of people. Emigration–immigration must be analyzed and understood within the specific social, political, and economic imperatives of the country that facilitates an exodus of people and a receiving country that welcomes them to settle within its borders. Saying that all Canadians are immigrants is an oversimplification of the idea that at some time in history, we all came from somewhere else.

The authors of *Multiculturalism and Ethnic Attitudes in Canada* obscured important distinctions when they stated we were all immigrants. So did Rosemary Brown, a New Democratic Party (NDP) member of British Columbia's Legislative Assembly through most of the 1970s. She began her speech to the Second Canadian Conference on Multiculturalism by addressing everyone present in this manner: "Fellow immigrants, descendants of immigrants, and descendants of descendants of immigrants ..."[2] Her point was clear: that we all came from somewhere outside Canada, and therefore we are all immigrants. Although this tired bromide is typically intended as a benevolent acknowledgement of our equal rights, it does not include the specific social reality of each wave of migration to Canada. The settling of the Canadian territory by Natives who had crossed the Bering Strait is certainly different from the coming of the British and French as colonizers and settlers, and both are distinct from the immigration of the nineteenth and twentieth centuries. Each of these phases takes place within a specific social, political, and economic context, which makes them different in their nature; each will have a different set of implications for Canadian society.

Canada's Migrations

The first human occupation of what would come to be known as Canada was by Native peoples. Their migration was not the result of individual decisions, as migration to Canada is today. Neither was it directed by an outside state, a mother country, as in the case of the French and the British settlers. Instead, it was a collective decision by people who inhabited the continent of Asia. Their basic objective was to settle in an unpopulated land and set up a social structure and economic system that would help them function in their new environment. They managed this successfully, and their success endured until the coming of the Europeans.

The second phase of migration from Europe was markedly different. The French and English first came for profit and conquest, and to reach their goals, they subjugated the Native peoples. As we know, they were all too successful. They uprooted Native cultures, dehumanized Native peoples, rendered their culture insignificant, and barely tolerated their existence.

This conquest was soon followed by a larger influx of French and English people needed for the settlement of the Canadian territory.

Although the original conquest did not require a great number of people, settlers were needed to sustain it. Migration became state policy for France and England, and both directed large numbers of their nationals to populate colonies that promoted their financial and cultural interests. They set up a society with close links to the mother countries and with institutions modelled on those in their former homeland. From the time of their arrival, they imposed their social model on the new land as much as the new environment would permit.

These two groups of original European settlers had a particular task and developed a special relationship with one another in Canada. They were fundamental to determining the type of society Canada would become, and their founding roles were officially recognized in the *British North America Act*, quite unlike that of the later immigrants, who came to increase the potential socio-economic development of an already established nation. The individuals who made up the original and the later-arriving groups might have had similar motivation for relocating, but this similarity mattered little because the question of Canada had already been settled. Simply put, they dealt with different historical and social realities.

Although the first settlers had come to form and shape a new society, those who followed would encounter a society whose primary institutions and basic social organizations had already been set up. Their role relative to the new society differed greatly. One came to build an economic structure for its socio-political companion, while the latter immigrants would come primarily as the labour pool to feed an expanding industrial complex. The first created the template of the new society. The second animated it by working in the mines, railroads, factories and, ultimately, the service industry. These significant differences cannot be glossed over.

This is not to diminish the role immigrants have had in building Canada. On the contrary, latter immigrants' contribution to the building of Canadian society is at least equal to that of the founding groups. We must recognize, however, that being equal contributors to the building of a society is not the same as having had equal roles in shaping it. The French and English had already shaped Canadian society according to their vision and interests prior to the others' arrival. Today the character of the nation's institutions, including its laws and cultural traditions, continue to reflect this difference. Recognizing this reality is critical to understanding the distinction between Native Canadians, early settlers, and later newcomers. It is far too simplistic to say we are all immigrants, descendants of earlier immigrants, or descendants of newer immigrants.

This does not mean immigrants as individuals or groups do not have similar fundamental rights to the two founding groups to create change in society in keeping with their wishes and interests. On the contrary, immigrants — precisely because of the tremendous contribution they have made — have every right to influence Canadian institutions. Neither can we say Canadian society should not change in keeping with new needs. Even the least open and democratic society must adapt to new social dynamics. The more open and democratic a society is, the more it should allow itself to be shaped by evolving social processes. No society can flourish without changing. The formation of a society is a continuous process, and society restructures itself according to constantly emerging social needs. Still, the basic nature of a society cannot change. The fundamental character given to Canadian society by the English and French, including its languages, institutions, and culture, retains its weight and historical significance. The struggle by immigrant groups to assert their visions and interests within Canada must be waged in full consideration of this historical reality.

Recognizing this fact, Charles Caccia, the Liberal representative for Davenport — a Toronto district with a high percentage of ethnic voters — said this in the early debate on the policy of multiculturalism:

> It strikes me as being significant that today's debate [on multiculturalism] has taken place so far in English and French, not in Ojibway, not in Italian, not in Polish, not in Ukrainian, not in Greek, and not in Portuguese. This has a certain significance. If the honourable member had spoken in Ukrainian in making his opening remarks, if the minister of state had replied in Polish and had been followed by the next member speaking Jewish and then by me speaking Italian, perhaps we would have been achieving real multiculturalism. The fact remains that we are addressing each other in this debate today either in English or French, and this is something that strikes me as being a fact of life in the country.[3]

This statement by the MP from Toronto points to the official status assigned to French and English, which other languages lack. Naturally, it is not just a question of language. Instead, it is the entire character of Canadian society in which these two groups have acted as founders while the later immigrants have inserted themselves within the established foundations. Metaphorically speaking, if we look at Canadian society as an edifice, we can say that the French and the English have been the architects and engineers who have designed its shape and structure, while the immigrants have been the hired labour for the further realization of the project.

To claim that we are all immigrants confuses our understanding of the history of immigration as a world phenomenon and leads us to an incorrect awareness of the different roles that the different phases of migration have had in building Canadian society. Recognizing these differences is critical to the distinction we want to make between Native Canadians, early settlers, and later newcomers. The assumption that we are all immigrants, or descendants of immigrants, or descendants of later ones, is not correct. It is obvious that political programs formulated to deal with immigrant groups need to recognize and accept these realities.

Chapter 5

Assumptions About Ethnicity

Within the last couple of decades, social scientists, government officials, and politicians have come to recognize ethnicity as an important issue. The ethnic question has pushed itself to the forefront of social and political debates and demanded that social and political activists take note. This means ethnic groups have to be acknowledged not only as demographic categories but as social groupings, with their own social and political agendas. It also means politicians who want to be elected need to incorporate the wishes and aspirations of ethnic voters into their political programs. In other words, since the 1960s we have witnessed an affirmation of ethnic politics.

This is quite a turnabout from the 1950s and earlier, when ethnicity was regarded as a transient phenomenon. It was believed that ethnic affiliation was a relic of the past and modern society would generate technocratic values that would render ethnicity moot. Further, it was believed that in a modern post-war state, technology itself would propagate the values of the dominant culture and, in time, effectively pave over the specific cultural values of ethnic groups. However, such predictions have not entirely materialized.

While in some countries, ethnicity undoubtedly no longer carries political weight, in others it is an undeniably critical consideration — one that politicians cannot push aside.

In Canada, ethnic populations are socially and politically present and demanding a larger role. The fact that we have a policy specifically regarding multiculturalism is an acknowledgement of their presence and activism in Canadian society. However, complex and potentially controversial questions swirl around even this simple fact. Who do we consider ethnic? What is an ethnic group? What percentage of the population is composed of people we consider to be ethnic? Do we also have a mainstream Canadian group that cannot be ethnically categorized?

The answers to such questions should define what we have in Canadian society and indicate what direction we would like Canadian society to take on the issue. As we have seen, for adherents of the mosaic model, Canadian society is made up of different ethnic components, each acting within its own social and cultural boundaries and operating in its own "solitude." Further, all Canadians are considered to belong to one ethnic group or another. This conflicts considerably with our point of view. It's true that ethnic aggregations do exist in Canadian society, but we cannot say all Canadians are ethnics, nor that they constitute groups that form an ethnic mosaic. If it is true that ethnic aggregations exist, it is also true that a vast number of people do not consider themselves ethnic and are part of the mainstream without any ethnic identification.

The divergence between our views and those held by theorists of the mosaic is rooted in the definition of ethnicity. Theorists of the mosaic establish ethnicity according to objective factors such as the ancestral line and use primordial factors to assign ethnic alliance and determine ethnic group formation. For us, ethnicity cannot be established by objective measurements or primordial factors. Instead, we consider the subjective inclinations of a person to be the prime factor for determining his or her ethnicity. We believe such inclinations to be the result of social and political imperatives. In other words, the determination is situational, although we certainly recognize the important roles that transmitted cultural views and ascriptions play in determining ethnic group affiliation.

Let us now analyze the assumption made by ideologists of the mosaic as it pertains to ethnicity and the formation of ethnic groups.

Who Is an Ethnic?

Closely associated with the incorrect assumption that everyone in Canada is an immigrant or has immigrant ancestors is the assumption, particularly essential to the ideologists of the mosaic, that all Canadians are ethnics. The mosaic adherents' logic is simple, linear, and mistaken. They maintain that everyone in Canada has, at some point in their family history, come from different parts of the world, carrying with them ethnocultural and racial backgrounds that reproduce themselves in Canadian society. Consequently, to speak of a free-standing Canadian identity is meaningless. Hence the hyphenated phenomenon: Native-Canadian, English-Canadian, French-Canadian, Ukrainian-Canadian, and so on. Within this vision of Canadian society, an individual's identity must be derived from ethnocultural lines, and if one's "roots" are unclear, his or her obligation is to rediscover what the years of living in Canada have blurred out.

This approach to finding our own ethnic identities illustrated itself in 1984, when the federal Ministry of Multiculturalism promoted a festival at Toronto's Roy Thomson Hall. A musical play was chosen as the medium to illustrate the quest for ethnic identity. The play's setting is a classroom in an ideal Canadian school — here also presented as a typical one — where everyone contributes to the positive nature of ethnic diversity. Everyone is co-operative: there is no racism and no conflict between teachers, administrators, and students — only universal admiration for the expressed ethnic differences of the school's population. If this was meant to represent a typical Canadian school, it certainly missed the mark, ignoring open racism, ethnic gang violence, and the all-too-frequent streaming of immigrant children into less academically oriented courses.

Still, let us look at what happens in this portrayal of a Canadian school regarding the question of ethnic identity. Over the duration of a school day, students express their outward ethnic identities through various social activities. But in the play, there is a problem: two students do not have any particular ethnic identity. One, a young woman, is quite upset by this apparent deficit and repeatedly asks, "Who am I?" while the other could not care less about his ancestral background.

These two students cannot be left without the all-important ethnic identity. It is the play's central conflict. Somehow the students must find out who they are, and indeed they do. At the climax of the play, we learn that the young woman, with the help of a computer, has traced her complicated ancestry and discovered her ethnic identity. In the denouement we see her in full Spanish costume. She is now a Spanish-Canadian. Meanwhile, the young man who had not cared about his ancestry is compelled by peer pressure to trace his ancestral background. In the end, he comes out in a Scottish kilt, and we assume everyone lives happily ever after.

The moral of the play is painfully evident. The school represents the ideal vision of Canadian society as defined by adherents of the mosaic theory: In the school, as in Canadian society, we are all ethnic and all of us behave in distinguishable ethnic ways. The school's administration represents the Canadian government, working to coordinate harmonious social behaviour among all the ethnic groups. In this metaphor, social scientists are also represented. Just as the computer helps one student to discover her ethnic background by navigating the intricate maze of her ancestry, sympathetic social scientists perform a similar function. They advise, help, and facilitate the tidy categorization and grouping of Canada's population by ethnic background.

The method used by many social scientists to categorize people and to appraise their social behaviour by ethnicity is based on ancestry and primordialism. For example, University of Toronto sociologist Wsevolod Isajiw, a member of the Canadian Ethnic Studies Association, made full use of this method to explain ethnic persistence in Canada. According to Isajiw, ethnicity in Canada can be explained through deep-seated, inalterable atavistic allegiances. In such a model, primordial feelings are so strong and blood lines so thick that they prevent ethnic identity from ever diluting. Consequently, under this view, when one asks, "Who am I ethnically?", the answer is always to be found in one's ancestral line.

This kind of thinking fuels the assumption that all Canadians are ethnics. The Census of 1971, the same year the policy of multiculturalism was adopted, suggested that everyone in Canada was ethnic, finding that 44.62 percent of the Canadian population was British, 28.03 percent French, 6.11 percent German, 3.39 percent Italian, and so on, to ever-diminishing but highly specific percentages, until 100 percent of the Canadian population was ethnically accounted for. These findings, reached by tracing ancestral lines, appeared to confirm the assumption that we are all ethnics. It answered for everyone who they were ethnically. In this way, the problem facing the young woman in the government-sponsored musical play vanishes. Her apparent ethnic identity crisis is resolved by genealogy, as it is for everyone, permitting the cast of an entire nation to move happily into their proper places in the mosaic.

The interesting thing about this Census and others like it is that by using ancestral lineage to categorize everyone's ethnicity, it disregards the subjective feelings of people regarding their own ethnic identities. It also fails to ascribe any importance to the expressed cultural values of the people in question. It simply assumes that people culturally express themselves according to their ancestry. It does not consider that although a person may have a last name belonging to a specific ethnic category, he or she might not share any social characteristics with others in the same category. As sociologist James McKay from Australia's University of Queensland points out, "Man," through this deterministic approach, "is seen as a leopard who cannot change his ethnic spots."[1] It does not allow for any social flexibility in response to the demands of a particular situation. Further, this method repudiates the vital role of women. It denies the role of women — unless, of course, we assume that all marriages are endogenous. Categorizing a person ethnically through the ancestral line by using a person's surname, considering that children generally take their father's last name, denies women any role in projecting a particular ethnicity. If ethnic differentiations mean differences in beliefs, customs, and values, surely women play at least an equal part in transmitting these values to their children.

The ancestral-line approach to categorizing people may have some value as a starting point for an ethnic social analysis, and certainly ancestry can be an important factor in determining one's ethnicity. However, relying on it exclusively, as the ideologists of the mosaic do, is incorrect. It does not do justice to the social accommodation that people living in Canada have sought and won for themselves. Further, it is an injustice against those who are the object of this sort of categorizing, when they may well consider their ethnicity to be different from what their surnames suggest.

It seems that an ethnic categorization of Canada's population needs to begin by giving full scope to people's subjective consideration of themselves. Their cultural lives would also need to be considered, along with their cultural and social aspirations. Their ancestry would certainly need to be given consideration, but it could not be the sole factor. Instead, the ideologists of the mosaic assume all Canadians can be ethnically categorized according to the ancestry suggested by their surnames.

The Ethnic Group

We have discussed how the ancestral approach has been used to categorize the ethnic identity of Canada's population and how this misrepresents the subjective inclinations of people as social actors by locking them into predetermined ethnic slots. We need also to understand that categorizing oneself ethnically is not necessarily the same as being part of an ethnic group. Becoming part of a group is possible only if certain needs, aspirations, and a sense of belonging are provided by the group itself.

Unfortunately, much of the sociological literature on ethnicity does not make a clear distinction between ethnic categories and ethnic groups. The terms are often used interchangeably, creating the impression that once a certain number of people are given a particular ethnic identification, this collection of people constitutes an ethnic group. In the article "Ethnicity and Ethnic Groups in America," M.G. Smith of Yale University points out that "almost always in the contemporary literature, ethnic units or aggregates are designated as 'ethnic groups' without the least pause or hesitation to consider whether or not they exhibit those qualities and characteristics that are normally associated with the concept of a group in social sciences."[2] Similarly for us, this association is untenable. Although most ethnic aggregates are labelled ethnic groups, they do not meet such a standard. Let us now discuss the differentiation between an ethnic category and an ethnic group.

It is necessary to test the assumption by ideologists of the mosaic that all Canadians are ethnics and that they come together to form ethnic groups in the Canadian mosaic. We must know what is meant by a social category and what constitutes a social group. As M.G. Smith points out, a social category "is simply an aggregate differentiated by one or more criteria which lacks the organization distinguishing a group. For example, American redheads will remain a category until they create an inclusive representative association to coordinate and represent their interests."[3]

Similarly, when we say that in Canada we have English-Canadians, French-Canadians, Italian-Canadians, etc., we cannot assume these people form distinct ethnic groups. Associating one with the other is a leap that does not consider the social processes necessary before these groups can constitute ethnic social entities.

Certain things need to happen for a number of people, ethnically categorized, to constitute a social group. First, such people need to have an awareness of their ethnicity. That is to say, they need to know they share ethnic traits that distinguish them from others. Although it is important to determine the awareness of one's ethnicity and slot oneself into a specific category, this constitutes only an elementary degree of ethnicity. This is marginal to one's essential role within a particular social context. These individuals need to pass from their state of ethnic awareness to one of being conscious of their ethnicity. The difference is that for the first, ethnic traits are only marginally important, while for the ethnically conscious, the same traits assume considerable importance. It will be evidenced by having strong sentiments about such differences and by a mentality of "us" versus "them." Being part of an ethnic group is a major determinant of social interactions. Third, ethnically conscious people need ethnic social structures that permit them to act out their perceived differences. These elements — ethnic consciousness and ethnic social structures — are mutually inclusive. The stronger the ethnic structures, the greater the possibility of reinforcing one's consciousness, and the greater the degree of consciousness, the more abundant the opportunities for creating channels to express the felt differences.[4] We need to determine what those channels are, what is required to constitute an ethnic group, and how such a group functions and takes care of its people.

We must look at what institutions exist and determine whether they satisfy the needs and expectations of ethnically conscious individuals. Does the group provide, as Raymond Breton of the University of Toronto calls it, "institutional completeness"?[5] In other words, are the individuals' social needs met by the institutions of their ethnicity? Does the group have places of worship, recreational clubs, cultural organizations, funeral homes, shopping centres, media, and other resources needed for people to interact effectively? Even more important, does it have schools or other institutions that can transmit ethnic culture and language to its children?

Implicit in our reasoning here is the notion that the existence of both ethnic awareness and consciousness does not automatically constitute a socially active ethnic group. In fact, it is possible to have a high degree of ethnic consciousness and yet not have institutions to guarantee the ability to interact socially with members of one's own group.

Having the potential to facilitate the social needs of a group depends on several factors. Primary among them is the size and concentration of the group. A small group of ethnically conscious people is not likely, in typical circumstances, to set up its own institutions. In such cases, the financial resources that could be generated by ethnic activities, businesses, or fundraising would not be enough to establish places of worship or social halls, for example, nor to sustain an ethnic newspaper or radio station. Neither would small groups have the human resources to administer their own institutions. The other question relates to the distribution of a particular number of ethnically conscious people. Being dispersed over a vast metropolitan area, or even across the country, precludes coming together.

It would appear that people in an ethnic category cannot automatically be considered an ethnic group. Instead, it would seem an ethnic group can exist only when a number of ethnically conscious people are able to interact socially on the basis of their ethnicity and can do so in institutions they have created for themselves, which reflect their uniqueness.

On the basis of this definition, it should be possible to look at each ethnic category within Canada's population and determine with some certainty whether it constitutes an ethnic group. It is not our goal to do this here, and neither do we have the means to do it. Still, we can draw some general conclusions based on our methodology and our observations of ethnicity at work in Canadian society. This would add some concreteness to our discussion. Before that, though, we must make one more clarification.

Briefly, we want to make a distinction between ethnic groups and national ethnic groups. This will help us to differentiate between ethnic groups such as Native Canadians, Quebecois, and other ethnic groups that may exist as the result of immigration. Establishing this difference is crucial for understanding the possible demands that each of these two groups — ethnic groups and national ethnic groups — can make on Canadian society and the ways these demands can be met.

We have classified an ethnic group based on its ability to sustain social institutions that meet the needs of its aggregates. In this sense, a national ethnic group is similar: it enables its people to act out their social interests in the institutions they have created for themselves. However, there is a fundamental difference between the two. The ethnic group does not have the ability to create its own political, judicial, and economic systems to sustain and regulate the lives of its members. In other words, the ethnic group cannot simply establish its own state. The national ethnic group, on the other hand, has enough resources to establish its own judicial, social, and political systems. It is possible for the national ethnic group, at least in theory, to construct its own state.

It is not our intention to lay out the criteria for determining the differences between the two. However, it demands more than looking at the aspirations of some or even most members of an ethnic group. As important as this may be, other, more objective factors need to be brought to the fore, such as the group's historic role in nation building, its economic life, its demography, and the range of its social and cultural institutions.

Canada's Ethnic Map

We have so far drawn distinctions between an ethnic category, an ethnic group, and a national ethnic group. We have pointed out in a theoretical way that an ethnic category is not necessarily an ethnic group, and that a differentiation exists between an ethnic group and a national ethnic group. Let us now illustrate our position with some examples drawn from Canadian society.

Our task, as we stated earlier, is not to draw an ethnic map of Canada by pointing out all the existing ethnic categories, which of these categories are in effect ethnic groups, and which are national ethnic ones. We want a theoretical mapping of this. We want to point out in general, by means of selected examples, the components of Canadian society regarding ethnicity. In other words, metaphorically speaking, our task is not to point out how many mountains, valleys, or hills exist in Canada but to differentiate between these land formations and be able to state, through general observation, whether mountains, valleys, and hills in fact exist.

We have seen that there are ethnic categories that cannot necessarily form themselves into ethnic groups, a transformation that requires more than ethnic consciousness among its members. It demands recognizing the possibility of acting out their ethnicity. Through this approach, it becomes clear to us that in Canadian society we have many people who could regard themselves as ethnic but do not have the opportunity to behave as members of ethnic groups.

Examples of this are not difficult to find. One has only to look at the scattered pockets of people who can be ethnically categorized but cannot come together as groups. Without sufficient numbers and concentration, a vital group with its own institutions cannot form. In such cases, ethnicity is often only symbolic. For example, can we say that the Turks in Canada, or the Maltese, truly constitute ethnic groups, with their own institutions and operating within closely knit communities? It is very unlikely that conditions for these two ethnic categories will change unless many more immigrants from Turkey and Malta enter the country. These people, although they might have a high degree of ethnic consciousness and wish to act out their ethnicity socially, would be unable to do so. Their ethnicity would remain largely private, confined to their families.

Such situations are not limited to people from small ethnic categories. People from larger ones can have the same difficulties in establishing their social units. For example, Italians, Germans, and Ukrainians who are part of large ethnic categories will sometimes encounter similar obstacles. Certainly, Italians in some areas of Toronto, or Germans in Kitchener, or Ukrainians in some cities of western Canada might be able to set up some institutions that transmit some of their culture. But what about an Italian or a few Italians who might live, say, in some parts of western Canada, or Germans in northern B.C., or Ukrainians in Nova Scotia? What kind of community institutions will they be able to support? How are they going to act out their ethnicity? Although such people might be ethnically conscious and want to live out their ethnicity, they will not be able to do so.

This does not imply that ethnic associations, organizations, and units do not exist in Canada. In fact, they have long been part of Canadian society, and will continue to play a considerable role in the cultural, economic, and political life of the country. One has only to look at existing ethnic organizations to figure out that the social expression of ethnicity is occurring in Canadian society. Ethnic places of worship, schools, political lobbies, and the expanding ethnic media are all indicators pointing to the vitality of ethnic groups and their respective communities.

The point here is not that ethnic organizations do not exist, but that we need to look at them and see to what degree they can serve the many facets of their communities. Can these units exist entirely on their own? Do they have the resources, numbers, and cohesion, or are they merely places for categories of ethnics to gather? What we need to look at is the vitality, completeness, and sustainability of an ethnic aggregation to determine if it is a viable ethnic group. Considering the ephemeral state of some ethnic social and cultural infrastructure, we wonder how far they will proceed in establishing themselves as durable, functioning groups.

In our attempt to designate what we have in Canada as ethnic categories and ethnic groups, we also want to consider national ethnic groups. Their histories have placed them in a different social context. We disagree with the assumption made by ideologists of the mosaic that each ethnic category represents a place in the Canadian ethnic mosaic. Mosaic adherents fail to understand the fundamental differences between ethnic groups and national ethnic groups. Can we equate the rights and aspirations of ethnic aggregations such as Italian-Canadians, Chinese-Canadians, or

German-Canadians with those of French-Canadians and Native Canadians? Even a cursory look at our history will tell us the answer is in the negative.

We have already pointed out that French-Canadians did not come as immigrants, but as settlers and colonizers, and Canada might well be a French-majority country today were it not for the outcome of a single battle. Although the English defeated the French militarily, they were not able to defeat the social, cultural, and economic institutions of the French-Canadians. In fact, the *British North America Act* recognizes the dual nature of Canadian society: French-Canadians with their own social, cultural, and political institutions, and English-Canadians with theirs. This duality has persisted up to the present. Certainly, we must recognize that there are marked differences between groups of people who have set up a society with a legal, cultural, and linguistic system congruent with their interests and views, and other people from different ethnicities who have entered a country where all the major institutions already have a definite character.

Another point that distinguishes French-Canadians from other ethnic groups is their geographic concentration. Although some ethnic groups might have most of their members in a particular area, the demarcation between them and others is not typically identifiable. Let us take Italian-Canadians as an example. If we look at this ethnic group, we see that it exists not just in one area of Canada, but in many major Canadian centres: Toronto, Montreal, Vancouver, Hamilton, and so on. Second, we note that there is no clear line separating their community from others. The point is that there is a clear difference between French-Canadians living mainly in a province that can be identified as theirs and other ethnic groups that are scattered throughout the country. French-Canadians in Quebec, among other things, could set up their own jurisdictional boundaries along clear geographical demarcations, while others could not.[6]

This distinction, along with different historical roles French-Canadians have had, could lead the French-Canadians to establish their own viable nation. Whether they will do so, or whether this is desirable, is another question. However, we must recognize that the potential exists. The very fact that French-Canadians in Quebec have a strong separatist movement indicates there are powerful political, economic, and cultural forces at play and that the formation of a Quebecois state is a real possibility. For other ethnic groups in Canada, such a possibility is not even thinkable. Most ethnics cannot even come together as true groups, and even when they do, they can barely support the few institutions that would sustain some degree of cultural continuity.

This fundamental difference can also be appreciated when we compare ethnic groups with Native Canadians. Although their group is in a situation different from that of French-Canadians, they can also lay claim to a different set of rights, which other ethnic groups cannot. This autochthonous population has been deprived of its own land. It has been confined to reserves or compelled to become like the "white man" in cities, and it has lost its ability to direct and shape its own destiny. Their struggle is like that of the other ethnics only insofar as they would like to carry on with their cultural traditions, but it goes much further. They want to reclaim large portions of their traditional lands and reconstruct their own societies according to their own cultural and social aspirations, independent of the non-Native population.

If we adhere to the ideology of the mosaic, such differentiations cannot be made. According to ideologists of the mosaic, we are all ethnics, and the rights and aspirations of one are similar to those of all others. This vision has a levelling effect — not by ascribing more rights to ethnic aggregates, but by reducing those of national ethnic groups. Is it at all surprising, then, to find French-Canadians and Native Canadians strongly rejecting the policy of multiculturalism when it is interpreted in this fashion? It does equal disservice to ethnic aggregates, potential ethnic groups, and national ethnic groups. For ethnic aggregates and potential ethnic groups, it risks creating unrealistic expectations, while diminishing the aspirations of national ethnic groups. Similarities between the rights of all groups certainly exist, but so do substantial differences. University of Toronto sociologist Jeffrey Reitz states, "In fact, although these groups formed by conquest have some attributes in common with other ethnic groups, they often resist this label, preferring to think of themselves as nations instead."[7]

The most significant dispute we have with ideologists of the mosaic is that they seek to obscure the reality of Canadian society. They do not recognize the differences that exist between ethnic categories, ethnic groups, and national ethnic groups. They consider them all similar and proceed to slot them into place like tiles of the mosaic. Further, by claiming we are all ethnic, they obscure the fact that many people prefer to live simply as Canadians.

Following the distinctions we make between an ethnic category, an ethnic group, and a national group, our view varies considerably from that of proponents of the mosaic theory. Certainly, ethnic communities exist in Canadian society, even if their size is sometimes exaggerated by ethnic enthusiasts, but we do not accept that a person's surname alone is proof of their ethnicity. We do recognize that ethnic categories exist but believe membership should be based on subjective personal inclination and not simply on primordial connection. These categories of ethnics could possibly form social organizations to represent their interests and perhaps constitute themselves as groups, but lack the resources, numbers, and concentration to allow them to form viable groups.

We recognize visible and practised ethnicity in Canada, but we also recognize the limitations that face some aggregations in coming together as organized groups. Even more important, we maintain that a Canadian ethnic mosaic does not exist. We see Canadian society as being composed of ethnic categories, ethnic aggregations, and national ethnic groups, together with a large number of people who profess no ethnic identity and function simply as Canadians.

Chapter 6

Mainstream Canadians

To accept the assumption that we are all ethnic is to deny that a mainstream Canada exists. In fact, most literature dealing with Canadian ethnicity is oblivious to the existence of a mainstream group and insists on slotting all people into ethnic categories according to their surnames. This is a false representation of Canadian society. In the process of analyzing Canadian ethnicity, we have seen that while some people who identify as ethnic can function as — or have the potential to function as — a group, others are just categories with no possibility of acting out their ethnicities. We have also argued that an ethnic category cannot be determined only by a person's last name and that one's subjective inclinations also need to be considered. In fact, if we were to do just that, a remarkable number of people would say simply that they are Canadian, making no further distinction.

In a survey asking Canadians about their ethnicity, John W. Berry and Rudolf Kalin of Queen's University and Donald K. Taylor of McGill University found that 59 percent of all respondents classified themselves simply as Canadian. Even more interesting, their survey also revealed that of those people whose ancestors are not English or French, only 12 percent indicated an ethnicity.[1] This is markedly different from the view held by the ideologists of the mosaic who maintain, using paternal ancestral lines, that 44.5 percent of Canadians are English-Canadians, 28 per cent French-Canadians, and 26.7 percent describe themselves as belonging to "other" ethnic groups. To the mosaic-minded, when people claim simply to be Canadian, they display a contradiction between what they claim to be and what they really are. When such people act out socially beyond their mosaic-assigned ethnic institutions, adherents believe they have been absorbed by Anglo-Canadian social organizations, setting aside their true ethnicity and displaying false consciousness. For ideologists of the mosaic who reason this way, the policy of multiculturalism is an instrument that could be used to awaken large pockets of repressed ethnicity. They believe multiculturalism could encourage each and every Canadian to return to his or her ethnic fold.

Our argument is that there is no false consciousness. Those who consider themselves simply Canadian channel their social action through the non-ethnic institutions that reflect their sincere interest in living in mainstream Canada. If it is true that ethnics exist in Canadian society, it is also true that a vast number of people see themselves simply as Canadian. This means that their work, leisure, and culture are not expressed through ethnic institutions, but through institutions that do not have any specific ethnic label. They do not get their news from specific ethnic media or belong to ethnic congregations or ethnic community halls. They don't participate in ethnic celebrations or cultural festivals. To group such people according to their fathers' ancestral lines is false.

Implicit in the ideological position of the mosaic is a denial of the existence of non-ethnic institutions. It is obvious that if we accept that all Canadians are ethnic and that each ethnic group operates within its piece of the mosaic, then all institutions in Canadian society must be ethnic. This has never been elaborated upon by the ideologists of the mosaic, but it is a logical inference. Following this line of thought, the CBC would be Anglo-Canadian, while Omni Television would be of the "other" ethnics. The *Globe and Mail* would be Anglo-Canadian, while *Corriere Canadese* would be Italian-Canadian. Schools are also regarded this way. The ideologists of the mosaic feel schools project an Anglo-Canadian cultural outlook. Consequently, the "other" ethnics need to establish educational institutions to reflect their ethnicities.

This type of reasoning is certainly evident in a number of recommendations made by some ethnic organizations and in some policies adopted by governing institutions. For example, in 1974 a report submitted to the Toronto Board of Education, *The Bias of Culture*, pointed out that Toronto schools de facto exclude non-English-Canadians from receiving the full potential of their education, as schools operate from Anglo cultural imperatives. The report hinted at a solution: creating alternative schools reflecting the specific cultural identities of every ethnic group.[2] The alternative-language schools proposal made to the Toronto Board of Education in the late 1970s was a direct result of this line of reasoning. Organizations claiming to represent the Armenian and Ukrainian communities asked the board to set up schools where the language of instruction would be Armenian and Ukrainian, respectively. The present heritage language policy, which attempts to allow schoolchildren to learn — for part of the school day — in their "own" language and within their "own" cultural ambience reflects that proposal. The motivation was to enable children to function within institutions that reflected their ethnic identities.

Does it really reflect their identities? Undoubtedly, Omni TV and *Corriere Canadese*, along with many other institutions, are in fact ethnic, as they cater to specific ethnic groups, but to categorize the CBC or the *Globe and Mail*, public schools, and other institutions — from private corporations to social clubs — as Anglo would not be entirely correct. Holders of this view would come to this conclusion based on the ancestral line of the people who compose them. If most are of British origin, they would label them as being Anglo-Canadian.

It is undoubtedly true that Canadian institutions are dominated by people whose ancestral line is British. The scholarly works of John Porter and Wallace Clement confirm the veracity of this statement. However, to assume from this observation that these institutions are Anglo-Canadian, as purveyors of the mosaic tend to do, is to make a mistake twice over. First, the assumption confers ethnicity based only on ancestry, which — as we have seen — is not correct. Second, it does not distinguish between institutions that are created for an ethnic group and those where people of a particular ethnicity may predominate. This distinction is essential, as it determines the types of strategies to be used to encourage ethnics to participate fully in Canadian society. If we believe the main institutions of the land belong to one particular ethnic group, then it would be essential for other ethnic groups to set up parallel institutions. On the other hand, if we recognize these institutions are not of a particular ethnic group, but merely dominated by people of a particular ancestry, different initiatives could help change their composition to help them become as heterogeneous as possible.

The question we need to ask at this point is this: Do mainstream institutions belong to the Anglo-Canadians, in the sense that they are of Anglos and for Anglos, or are they institutions in which people of English ancestry predominate? Wallace Clement, as we have noted, has demonstrated how the main economic institutions are dominated by people of English-Canadian ancestry. However, he has also noted that French-Canadians have an important influence and play important roles in them, as do Jewish-Canadians and other non-Anglo ethnics. It is just as important not to underestimate the ascending economic power of people of other ethnicities. For example, how do we view the economic power of Italian-Canadians who have large holdings in real estate, who own large construction firms, and have begun to penetrate other areas of the economic infrastructure of Canadian society? It is not ethnic businesses we are talking about here. Instead, we have in mind businesses that may have started, at the beginning of their settlement in Canadian society, specifically to serve an ethnic interest and to fill a vacuum left open by the established business, but that have now grown beyond "ethnic" proportions.

However, with figures on hand it can still be argued that the Canadian economic elite is primarily of a British ancestry and that this could reflect a discriminatory attitude toward people of non-British origin. We are the last to argue that discrimination does not exist in Canadian society. While it is true that ethnic representation among Canada's economic and social elites is disproportionately low, we must also examine this in the context of elites. Any elite group is such because it successfully prevents others from penetrating it. Consequently, it should be no surprise that this elite would keep others out, whether or not they are of the same ethnicity. Interesting studies could be undertaken to see whether such exclusion is based on ethnicity or other factors. We could possibly look at the vast numbers of English immigrants who came after the Second World War and compare the numbers of these who have penetrated the elite versus other immigrants who arrived at the same time. Unfortunately, no such study exists — at least to our knowledge. Our guess is that English immigrants from this period, although still having the advantage of a similar language, have simply not outdistanced others significantly enough to determine a difference.

Other points to consider, when we reflect on this low and slow penetration of the upper levels of Canadian society, are education, language, and economic conditions of groups of immigrants. Somehow, studies like those of Clement make conclusions without considering questions that could significantly influence the results.

For example, first, the financial resources of immigrants on arrival have not typically permitted them simply to step into Canada's upper socio-economic ranks. Second, first-generation immigrants have generally lacked the educational requirements to qualify them for more economically rewarding positions. Third, most immigrants have not come with sufficient fluency in English to win positions that matched their personal capabilities. It is difficult to imagine a first-generation immigrant with hardly any knowledge of English, little formal education, and no capital becoming a director of a top-tier financial institution.

It would seem that to develop a more accurate understanding of the degree of ethnic exclusion from elite institutions, ethnicity should be isolated from other factors. In other words, the role of ethnic differences in determining success should be considered only after eliminating other factors such as education, English proficiency, economic means, and other relevant influences. In the U.S., this approach has been used to prove that racism ultimately determines who is successful. Not surprisingly, when black and white Americans have been compared, whites have fared much better, even when all other relevant factors were the same. The fact that the elite are predominantly of a particular ethnic background does not prove discrimination based on ethnicity. In fact, the contrary could be argued. If we consider the lack of funds of many new immigrants, their limited fluency in English, or their subordinate social ranks in their countries of origin, the degree of immigrant success could actually be regarded as proof of the openness of Canadian society. Nonetheless, it remains the struggle of "other" ethnic groups to penetrate the higher echelons of Canadian institutions as their merit permits.

In the political arena, the situation is similar. It is pointless to deny the political influence of French-Canadians. Whether this degree of influence is proportionate to the number of French-Canadians in other arenas of Canadian life is another question, but for our point, it is enough to observe that in Quebec, there are political forces powerful enough to assure that French-Canadian interests and perspectives are protected at the national level. Still, there are economic, social, and political interests that feel that a separate nation, with its own institutions, needs to be established. Whether this is adequately done or not still has to be determined. Whatever the ultimate outcome, the fact remains that French-Canadians have a high degree of representation and influence in Canadian institutions, including Parliament, which has a long tradition of French-Canadian prime ministers and cabinet ministers.

Other people of different ethnicities — non-British and non-French — have also had important political roles, locally, provincially, and federally. We must not forget that Prime Minister John Diefenbaker was of neither British nor French background. He labelled himself simply as Canadian and his ancestry was German. Neither can we gloss over Edward Schreyer, also of German background, who was elected Premier of Manitoba and later appointed Governor General of Canada. Just as important is to note that some ministers are foreign born. For example, Charles Caccia, Minister of Labour and later Minister of the Environment in the Trudeau government, was born in Italy and came to Canada at an already mature age.

Let us leave aside these questions of ethnicity as they relate to the established economic, political, and cultural institutions, and look at everyday Canadians and the institutions that represent them, especially in their occupational, social, cultural, and recreational activities. Can we say the Canadian Labour Congress or the National Hockey League are English-Canadian? Certainly not. These organizations were not created to cater only to Canadians of British origin. Neither do they reflect a particularly British character. These organizations, like many others, have been created and developed in a Canadian context and cater to everyone who identifies with their objectives, regardless of their ancestral line. After all, it would be difficult to argue that the ethnic character of a hockey league is British when the sport is hardly known in Britain.

This leads to the second point we want to make when we consider whether Canadian institutions, be they national or local, are intentionally representing Anglo-Canadian culture. It should be obvious that if this were so, people of British ethnicity who want to protect their culture would not need to set up parallel organizations to represent their ethnic interests. University of Winnipeg historian Ross McCormack points out that English immigrants encountered the same difficulty as other newcomers adjusting to Canadian society. In fact, they did not recognize themselves in Canada's established cultural organizations and did feel the need to set up a network of social organizations to maintain their English-ness. Like other foreigners, they relied on family to provide emotional support and practised endogamy to support and safeguard shared cultural values. They also used chain migration and ended up in all-English boarding houses and hostels. McCormack further points out that the foundation of their social networks comprised Anglican churches, clubs, and lodges, which insulated them from Canadian society. Cultural societies of English immigrants such as the Sons of England, which in 1913 had more than forty thousand members in Canada, were created with the express purpose of promoting and maintaining English cultural views. This organization was fundamentally different from, let us say, the Canadian Labour Congress: although it might have predominantly members of English origin, it was created to advance a particular social interest common to a wide spectrum of Canadians.[3]

The distinction between organizations in which people of a particular ethnic origin dominate and those created by and for particular ethnic groups is crucial because it determines the types of political and social activities ethnics can undertake. For example, if an organization is exclusive to a particular ethnicity, then people of different ethnicities would need to create other organizations suited to their own ethnocultural interests. If this were to be so — that is, if all Canadian institutions were to have specific ethnic characteristics — then Canadians would need to establish and join ethnic groups reflecting their own ethnicities or form organizations that would permit them to behave according to their ethnocultural interests. This is what ideologists of the mosaic would prefer. The example we used earlier — of the young woman in the musical play at the multicultural festival — illustrates this position. The young woman, not knowing her ethnicity and having considered herself simply as a Canadian, is obliged by others to rediscover her past. These "others" could be regarded as the personification of the ideology of the mosaic. She finally discovers, through the use of a computer (read: social scientists), that one of her ancestors was Spanish. Having at last found her niche, she begins to dress, eat, and be socially active as a Spanish-Canadian.

On the other hand, if we also have social, political, recreational, and economic institutions that, instead of catering to particular ethnicities, are more broadly of and for Canadians, another possibility is available. Those who cannot form themselves into ethnic groups, for reasons we have already discussed, or who are just catalogued into ethnic categories, have the liberty to be part of institutions and aggregations that are free from ethnic labels. People who still wish to see their ethnicities reflected in their social lives could, as we will discuss later, infuse these mainstream organizations with aspects of their ethnic lives.

In concrete terms, this distinction between institutions dominated by people of English ancestry and institutions made by and for English-Canadians leads us to ask a number of questions. Should ethnic groups concentrate on ensuring there is a full suite of parallel institutions, or should they try to bend mainstream organizations to their interests? Should ethnics who exist only in categories try to establish viable social groups where possible, or should they get involved in mainstream ones? What about those who do not see themselves as ethnic at all? Should they try to discover their ethnicities, or continue to live simply as Canadians? The answers are contingent on what our view of ethnicity is, on what constitutes an ethnic group, and on the flexibility and openness of the mainstream to incorporating differences.

Ideologists of the mosaic have easy answers. They simply state that all Canadians are ethnics and therefore all Canadian institutions are ethnically structured. We have seen how this view fails to consider that these institutions, although they may be dominated by people of British origin, are not composed only of British-Canadians. They are not of any particular ethnic group. We have seen that people who feel that they are of British ethnicity have had to organize themselves outside these institutions. We acknowledge that adherents of the mosaic do not accept that there can be mainstream institutions that are simply Canadian. We follow a different methodology for establishing ethnicity. We have seen that for proponents of the mosaic, ethnicity derives from a person's surname. We look at ethnicity as situational and dynamic and believe people retain or let go of their ethnicity for any number of reasons. Objective social factors and people's behaviour determine their ethnicity. We recognize that ethnic aggregates and ethnic groups sometimes create organizations to act out their ethnicities. Similarly, we see that a vast number of people do not regard themselves as ethnic at all and channel their social energies into institutions that are not ethnically oriented.

We have discussed the incorrectness of the assumption made by ideologists of the mosaic with respect to immigration and ethnicity and shown that mainstream institutions do exist. In our next section, we will examine the forms of both ethnic and mainstream cultures that exist in Canada.

Chapter 7

The Assumption of Culture

Crucial to understanding ethnicity in Canada is the question of culture. Still, as important as culture is for understanding the identities of ethnic groups, facilitating inter-ethnic relations, or determining the role ethnic cultures should play within the wider cultural context, it has never been given due attention. That is not to say that the notion of culture is not evoked in attempting to prove one case or another vis-à-vis ethnic groups. In fact, it is quite the opposite. Terms such as *ethnic cultural identity, cultural mosaic, ethnocultural group, multiculturalism*, and *cultural pluralism* are commonly used. Still, there is little clarity regarding what "culture" means in terms of ethnic groups. Such inattention has permitted a demagogic and instrumental use of the term.

The storyline goes something like this: Immigrants arrived with rich cultures, only to be assailed by the Anglo cultural tradition, which sought total assimilation. The immigrants resisted successfully and were able to establish their own cultural communities. This resistance has given Canada the many ethnic cultural groups that are the basis of the country's cultural plurality. This, in turn, has permitted children of immigrants to carry on the cultural traditions of their ancestors. This is a nice story, but it does not reflect the reality that has confronted immigrants' cultures as they came into contact with other cultures and, as newcomers, engaged with Canadian life as they found it.

The assumption that today's ethnic groups have vibrant cultures to pass along to their offspring reflects a particular way of looking at culture. Culture has been elevated to a quasi-metaphysical, esoteric abstraction. This does not allow us to look at the cultures that immigrants brought in terms of their adaptability to a new set of circumstances. It makes it possible to ignore the dialectical relationship that exists between socio-political and economic systems on one hand, and cultures on the other. Further, the dynamic relationship that develops between the immigrants' cultures and that of the host society and between the cultures of the immigrant groups themselves is also not considered. Somehow it is assumed that the original culture of the immigrants and its tools for communicating that culture, particularly its language, remain intact and capable of being preserved in the new society. This lack of analysis of the dynamics of cultures as they relate to one another leads us to the third incorrect assumption made by ideologists of the mosaic.

They operate within this mythical and abstract view of the nature of culture for Canada's ethnic groups. They do not see culture as something that evolves in response to the new social needs of immigrants and the different demands made on them. Instead, it is regarded as static and immutable because it is based on the immigrants' primordial nature.

This, again, is a nice idea, but again, cultures are not like vegetables that can be pickled and preserved on a shelf. Cultures change and adapt to new circumstances. If we look at culture this way, the absurdity of the ideologists' statements becomes clear. If those statements were true, it would mean that immigrants coming from different political or socio-economic systems, or societies with laws and values unlike Canada's laws and values, would be able to carry on their traditions in the midst of, let us say, Toronto — a metropolitan city in the heartland of a modern industrial society. Instead, we find that such people adapt to the values and norms of their new society. Whether they do this willingly, or whether this is positive or even desirable, are not questions to be raised here. The fact is people who have lived part of their lives in societies with different cultures have to change their ways if they want to survive in a new environment. Preserving their culture unchanged would not mean synchronizing to their new society, but being alienated from it.

Because culture, then, does not change according to the ideology of the mosaic, its proponents view Canadian culture as a mosaic-like formation, so that when we speak of culture in Canada, we do not speak of a uniform Canadian culture but only of a British-Canadian, French-Canadian, German-Canadian, or Italian-Canadian culture. This view does not take into consideration the transformation that a culture undergoes to adapt to a new environment and the demands that a new and different society makes on the holders of particular cultural values.

We have seen that in the eyes of ideologists of the mosaic, there is no Canadian mainstream group, and that the country's population is no more than a collection of hyphenated Canadians. Ideologists of the mosaic do not make references to Canadian culture, per se. Instead, they break it down into ethnocultural traditions. This is how, for example, Leo Driedger, in an introduction to a collection of articles generally celebrating the concept of the Canadian mosaic, describes the region of western Canada: "This is the only region where no group is in the majority, although the British form the largest group. The region is highly rural and agricultural; it includes substantial enclaves of British, German, Ukrainian, French, and small ethnic groups. Many promote British, Ukrainian, German, French, and other cultures, because no one group dominates the region culturally."[1] He goes on to describe other Canadian regions in a similar way, attributing particular ethnocultural characteristics to each. What is interesting in this analysis, and others like it, is that there is never any reference to a Canadian mainstream and its corresponding culture. It is logical that if ideologists of the mosaic were to accept that a Canadian mainstream society existed, they would also need to accept the existence of a mainstream Canadian culture. That different cultures have been brought over is obvious. However, the idea that these cultures have been preserved and have flourished is a different question, which needs to be looked at in the light of our understanding of culture.

Our Understanding of Culture

When we speak of culture, we typically use an anthropological definition. As we see in ethnic scholar Naomi R. White's article, "Ethnicity, Culture and Cultural Pluralism," we think of culture as "that complex whole which includes knowledge, belief, art, law, morals, customs and any other capabilities and habits acquired by men as a member of society."[2] In this definition are two implicit notions of culture. The first refers to culture in a more generalized way that deals with its values, while the second refers to its behavioural aspects.

When we talk about the values of a culture, we are dealing with types of orientation regarding themes, ideals, or common understandings that underlie the institutions of a given population. In other words, societies are described as operating within a framework of value orientations or shared meanings, which form the culture and its institutions.

If culture is understood this way, we may say there is a fundamental similarity between all groups living in Canada, in that no particular ethnic group challenges the fundamental values of Canadian institutions. Howard Brotz, in a refreshing article about

Canada's multicultural policy, argues this point convincingly. He points out that only Native Canadian culture seems to present a challenge to the liberal democratic, bourgeois character of our society.[3] The other group that challenges Canadian society, the Quebecois, does so not on the basis of a different value system, but only in political terms, which reflect a struggle over available resources. This being true does not mean, we want to add, that there is no challenge to the so-called bourgeois liberal democratic orientation of Canadian society. When such challenges emerge, as marginal as they may be, they do not come from any specific ethnic group but from sectors of the population that cannot be identified as any particular ethnicity.

We may say that as far as ethnic groups are concerned, their cultural values are relatively similar to each other and not unlike those of the wider Canadian society. A smooth functioning of our social system would not be possible otherwise. For example, Canadians value the use of technology, share a generally similar view of private property, and a similar appreciation for a democratic society. These are values that permeate Canadian society and permit our legal system to retain its legitimacy. If such legitimacy, based on shared cultural values, were not present, we could predict that people would rebel or revolt. In this sense, we can safely say there are no ethnic groups in Canada fomenting rebellion or forging revolution.

The second notion of culture implicit in Tylor's definition[4] refers to the behavioural patterns of people. By this it is meant the traditions, customs, and lifestyle that, although they may be anchored to the same cultural values, may vary from one group to another. For example, people of France share fundamental values with people of Italy in terms of religion, political ideology, and economic aspirations, but a distinction can still be witnessed in some cultural behaviour. This difference has, in turn, given rise to different traditions of artistic expressions through painting, music, dance, and literature. It is also expressed in two different, if related, languages, which are both tools for communicating the respective cultures and symbols.

Ideologists of the mosaic share with us the understanding that cultural behaviour, language, and artistic expression are inseparable. Their view is that the manifestation of different cultures is a fact of life in Canadian society, evidenced by observably different cultural behaviour and languages. We differ, however, when we compare the cultures that immigrants brought with them and the ways they have changed as those immigrants have adapted to life in Canada. In the minds of the mosaic theorists, these original cultures and languages have been preserved in Canadian society and accordingly they manifest themselves as different pieces of the cultural mosaic. This view, in our minds, rests on three fallacies. First, such ethnic cultures and languages have changed considerably from the ones originally brought over. Second, even those altered cultural behaviours and languages are doomed. They lack sufficient ethnic social structures and economic bases to sustain and propel them forward. Third, their position denies the existence of a Canadian cultural mainstream. We believe Canada has a distinct culture and unique character, one that can only be labelled Canadian.

Canada's Cultural Map

We have pointed out previously that not all of Canada's population is ethnic. In that discussion we indicated that ethnic categories and aggregations certainly do exist, and that given the proper conditions could form themselves into full-fledged ethnic groups. Such groups can exist only when a sufficient number and concentration of people are conscious of their ethnicity, are willing to act it out socially, and are able to do so because they have social structures that permit it. We have also pointed out that there are two national ethnic groups: the Quebecois and Native Canadians, who cannot be lumped together with other ethnic categories or groups owing to the distinct roles they have played and continue to play in Canadian society.

Our cultural map follows from this. What is implied when we say "acting an ethnicity out socially" is the notion of a demonstrable cultural behaviour. That is to say, if a group of people behaves differently from others, it may only mean their cultural behaviour is different, without necessarily differing from the higher aspect of culture: their value system. The difference between this understanding of the Canadian cultural reality and that of the ideologists of the mosaic is considerable. Apart from conflicting appraisals of what constitutes an ethnic culture and disagreement over the idea that the Quebecois and Native Canadians have different cultural, political, and economic expectations, a critical difference is that mosaic theorists do not recognize the existence of a cultural mainstream. For now, let us look at what constitutes an ethnic culture and how that differs from the vision of the mosaic.

The Culture of Ethnic Groups

In the preceding pages, we have pointed out the interdependence of language and culture and we have explained how culture cannot be understood outside the context of a society's economic base and infrastructure. We have further pointed out that cultures need a set of social institutions to sustain, develop, and transmit them. In the following pages, we will examine the nature of ethnic cultures and look at changes that may occur to immigrant cultures when their social and economic contexts are altered.

We start from the premise that immigrants bring with them cultural assets of which they do not dispose as they enter a new country. Immigration, as we pointed out in an earlier chapter, is an inflow of labour resources. Importing immigrants is, of course, far different from bringing in a simpler, concrete commodity like technology. The latter is devoid of any characteristics beyond what it has been designed for, while the former comes with all the rich, complex qualities that define humanity. In other words, the coming of immigrants to Canada means the coming of people with views, outlooks, and customs that reflect lives lived in other social circumstances. Immigrants' culture remains with them and is not disposed of as easily and quickly as some people would like.

The question is this: What happens to a culture when it enters a Canadian social setting that includes other cultures? Our view is that it changes considerably in the process of adjusting to new social and environmental conditions. A major component of culture that we can use as a barometer of these changes is language. We feel that language, as we have stated before, is a tool and a symbol of culture. It collects and reflects the changes a culture undergoes. Language and culture are interdependent. This makes language a useful tool for understanding what changes have taken place in the original cultures brought over by immigrants to Canada.

Cultural Values

We have tried to draw a distinction between cultural values, which encompass general principles of sociability, and cultural behaviour. Certainly, these are part of the cultural baggage immigrants bring with them. They bring not only general values emanating from their lived experiences and their visions of what society should be like, but also customs and traditions that express who they are. We will return to the behavioural aspect of culture, but in the meantime, let us discuss immigrants' baggage of cultural values — their value systems.

It is obvious that any society needs to have consensus on certain basic values if it is to function peacefully. When such consensus is lost, the result is social rebellion, or even revolution. In such cases, core values that have held a society together lose legitimacy. Immigrants entering a country that has been constituted in keeping with certain social values are expected to submit to the general principles of their new society. If not, they can be accused of posing a threat to the established order. It is tacitly understood by both parties — the immigrants and the host society — that the host society's guiding principles will be respected.

Despite this shared understanding, the Canadian government does take some precautions to ensure that immigrants will generally adapt to Canada's social expectations. For example, the Canadian government has frowned on people of the political far left becoming permanent residents, and it has been especially averse to avowed Communists entering Canada as immigrants. In the 1950s, large numbers of Italian immigrants were screened before leaving Italy, and those who declared themselves to be Communists, or who were pointed out to be such by the local authorities, were not given the required visas.

This does not mean that some immigrants have not ventured beyond the confines of social and political expectations. Many have been severely punished for doing so. We need only recall the notorious American case of anarchist Italian immigrants Nicola Sacco and Bartolomeo Vanzetti. As Vanzetti pointed out in his final speech to the court, they were not being executed for a crime (of which they were posthumously exonerated), but for being immigrants who had different values and a different vision of what American society should be like. Although this case featured just two individual immigrants, such persecution can be applied to an entire immigrant group. For example, the case of racist government policies against Chinese immigrants (the "Yellow Peril") in western Canada at the beginning of the twentieth century, and that of Japanese-Canadians being interned as national security threats during the Second World War, also prove this point. If society feels threatened by any particular immigrant group, measures may be taken that affect the entire group, regardless of fairness. The actions of the Canadian government against these two groups, although totally unjustified, were those of a society defending itself against a perceived threat to its integrity. The motivation for acting against these two groups might have had more to do with racism and economics, but the rationalization was that the Chinese were undermining the essence of Canada's society and the Japanese were potential fifth columnists. These incidents not only tell us of the extent of racism and xenophobia in Canadian society at that time, but they also illustrate how Canadian society may react if it feels threatened by a particular immigrant group.

Whether immigrants who are chosen to come to Canada already have cultural values similar to those of the host society, or whether they succumb to the pressures of Canadian society to accept them, the result is that the cultural values of different ethnic groups will not be permitted to vary substantially from those of the host society. It is a practical matter. Otherwise, we would be talking not about one Canadian society but a multitude of societies, each operating with its own particular brand of political, social, and cultural institutions. Only then would it be possible for us to speak of a real cultural pluralism. But as Brotz points out, this does not exist in Canada, as ethnic groups have channelled their goals and aspirations within what he calls a liberal bourgeois system.[5]

We have indicated that there are two components of culture: cultural values and cultural behaviour. One relates to general values of social cohabitation, the other to people's lifestyles. In relation to the first, we have argued that immigrant groups in Canada have generally accepted a social order that does not vary between ethnic groups and is not unlike that of other Canadians. In this sense, a truly culturally pluralistic society does not exist. This, however, does not mean that to speak of cultural pluralism in Canada is totally false. The question cannot be so easily dismissed. If we look at the other manifestation of culture, cultural behaviour, the situation is different. There are different lifestyles among Canada's people, expressed by the food we eat, the friends we make, and the forms of entertainment and recreation we choose. If we view culture as also including these features, then we can say that in Canada, different ethnocultural characteristics are displayed and that a sort of multicultural Canada does exist.

Although this may resemble the position of the mosaic ideologists in the sense of affirming ethnic cultures, our position is different. Our understanding of what constitutes an ethnocultural behaviour and how it develops is different. For us, a process takes place that inexorably brings the cultures of immigrants ever closer to the broad culture of other Canadians. Our priority here is to understand this process. Ideologists of the mosaic emphasize preservation. For them, the idea is that immigrants bring over cultures that remain vibrant within their particular tiles on the cultural mosaic and are capable of being transmitted to future generations. They are oblivious to the change that invariably happens to the original cultures of immigrants. For us, this is not so. Cultures adapt to new social circumstances facing immigrants, and new cultural behaviours develop. In turn, these cultural changes alter the original language of the immigrants, giving form to hybrid versions.

Chapter 8

Acculturation

Cultures, if they have extensive contact with others, will absorb traits previously foreign to them, developing characteristics that render them significantly different from their original form. This process is referred to as acculturation. As John Milton Yinger points out, acculturation "is the process of change toward greater cultural similarity brought about by contact between two or more groups."[1] A fair number of studies have dealt with this, and foremost among them is the work of Milton Gordon. In his work, *Assimilation in American Life*, he describes a process in which, although they retain some of their cultures, immigrant groups move toward a way of life similar to that of the American mainstream.[2]

Similarly interesting is the fieldwork of Carla Bianco, who made a study of two towns named Roseto, one in the U.S. and one in Italy. A large number of people from the Italian Roseto moved to the American Roseto. The study shows how the inhabitants of the American Roseto made considerable efforts to retain their original culture. They made sure everyone in the American Roseto had originated from the Italian Roseto. They established parallel social and cultural institutions to preserve their original culture. Still, when the cultural behaviour of the residents of the American Roseto was compared to the behaviour of residents of its Italian counterpart, the two were found to be different. A hybrid culture had developed in the American Roseto, and though some of its characteristics could be traced to the town in Italy, it had also incorporated many aspects of American life. The core Italian culture of the immigrants could not resist the influence of its American counterpart.[3]

A broader work of Patrick Gallo's, reflecting on the entire experience of the Italian-Americans, draws this conclusion: "The Anglo core culture could not be so hermetically sealed off from forty million immigrants. Just as the core culture introduced new concepts to the immigrant masses, so too the latter brought their own ideas and customs, [and] some of these were absorbed and not annihilated by the host culture."[4] The process of acculturation and intermingling of cultures, which has taken place in Canada and still continues, is not unlike what is described above. Immigrant groups have had to interact socially with other immigrants and the established core inhabitants, resulting in cultural changes to all sides.

Immigrants had to adapt to a new set of social demands and came into contact with different lifestyles upon arrival in Canada. In the process of adapting and learning to live with others with different customs, their cultural behaviour changes. Often these changes are unknown to the immigrants themselves, who believe they are carrying on as they always have. But the illusion is shattered when they get the opportunity to return to their countries of origin. It is usually a cultural shock — almost as intense as the one they first experienced when they came to Canada. They are abruptly confronted with a society that seems to have totally changed into one they cannot recognize. It is not unusual to hear such people pledge they will never make another trip to their "home" country as they find it so "crazy." It is certainly true their former countries have changed, because no society can remain frozen in time, but the immigrants themselves have also changed and become "crazy" in the eyes of friends and relatives who still live in their former countries.

Immigrants fashion for themselves a unique hybrid lifestyle. It features unaltered characteristics of their original cultures, characteristics that can be traced to their countries of origin but have changed in form and content, and characteristics derived entirely from the new country. Alan B. Anderson, in his study of Ukrainians living in Canada, finds their "contact with Canadians of other ethnic origins" has "meant irreversible acculturation."[5] Alexander Matejko makes the same point about Polish-Canadians: "Poles and other Slavs become more cosmopolitan in their general outlook following their socio-economic advancement, fluency in English, higher security, and the broader societal contacts outside their own ethnic group."[6]

If indeed a new cultural hybrid does take shape for immigrants, we should be able to observe it in their spoken language. Without going into a full analysis of linguistic mutations that occur in each immigrant group, we will draw on some observations about Ukrainian-Canadians and offer some examples of language mutations that occur in the language of Italian-Canadians, taken from our own experience as active members of this community. By doing this we do not intend to generalize about all ethnic groups in Canada. Each group, we feel, needs to be studied separately to determine the degree of acculturation and the corresponding language changes that have taken place.

Culture and language are integral to one another, so changes to one will mean changes to the other. This is so not only for languages that immigrants bring to a new country, but for any language. When we say present-day English is different from that of Chaucer, we are also implicitly stating that culture in England is different from its medieval period. The language reflects the changes. Because such a relationship exists between culture and language, the cultural hybrid we have talked about should have a counterpart hybrid language, and not the original language immigrants brought over.

Alan B. Anderson discusses the hybrid nature of the language spoken among Ukrainian-Canadians in Canada's western provinces. In the process of acculturation, he indicates that "considerable anglicization of Ukrainian dialects began to occur. Many new words derived from English were incorporated into the everyday language of Ukrainian-Canadians. English combined with Ukrainian was heard increasingly, and the second generation typically imposed Ukrainian verb conjugation and sentence structure on the English they had learned."[7]

The same phenomenon has taken place with the language spoken by French-Canadians in Quebec. Although, as we have pointed out, these people cannot be considered simply as another ethnic group; their language has undergone the same process. It is a combination of original French words they brought over, anglicized versions of many of these words, and English words made to sound French.

The situation has been similar for Italian-Canadians. The language spoken in homes today, with some very rare exceptions, is a combination of Italian words, words from particular Italian dialects, Italian words made to sound like English, and English words that are Italianized. But it is not just the mutation of words that takes place. Entire sentence structures change, often rendering the "Italian" spoken by these people incomprehensible to Italians in Italy.

Let us look at the changes that take place, using some widely used words as examples. The word *factory* in Italian is *fabbrica*, but Italian-Canadians typically use *fattoria*, which is simply the English word *factory* bent into an Italian-sounding one. Communication is further complicated by the fact that the word *fattoria* already exists in Italian, but means *farm*. Often, when Italian-Canadians want to inform a relative or friend in Italy that they work in a factory, the Italian misunderstands that they work on a farm. A similar problem of misunderstanding occurs with the word *camera*. In Italian the equivalent word is *macchina fotografica*, while the Italian word *camera* means *room* or *chamber*, and unintended meanings can lead to hilarious situations. Another example is the word for *car*. In Italian, the word is *automobile* or *macchina*, but Italian-Canadians say *carro*. The "ro" is added to make the English word sound Italian. This is similar for Spanish-speaking people living in Canada or the U.S. In Mexico, *car* is *coche*, but for Mexicans living in the English-speaking part of the continent, car becomes *carro*.

The changes immigrants make to their native languages go beyond words. Sometimes, even when they make great efforts to exclude hybrid words, immigrants' sentence construction can give them away. For example, often if Italian-Canadians want to say, "I heard it on television," they will make a literal translation from English and say, "*L'ho sentito sulla televisione*." To a native Italian speaker, this means, "I have heard it on top of the television." Other examples like these are endless.

In fact, the amalgamation of Italian and English, along with different words from various regional dialects, constitutes the language of Italian-Canadians. The Italian language the immigrants brought over changes from Italian to *Italiese* (Italian plus *Canadese* equals *Italiese*), a term employed by Gianrenzo Clivio, a linguistics professor at the University of Toronto. This is the popular everyday language spoken not only by second-generation Italian-Canadians when they are not using English, but also by the adapted first generation. The process of acculturation begins the minute an immigrant enters a new society and within weeks, Italian immigrants increasingly begin to use *Italiese*. The consequence is that the vast majority of Italian-Canadians either lose or never develop the ability to communicate in standard Italian, which becomes for them what Latin had become in medieval times: the language of an elite divorced from the popular languages of the people and from everyday culture.

Such linguistic mutations give form to a hybrid language, reflecting the cultural changes that immigrants have made in adapting to a new society and interacting with other cultures. The new cultural behaviour can be traced to their country of origin, but it is certainly nourished by their life experiences in a new environment. When they call for the preservation of heritage languages in their original form, ideologists of the mosaic do not consider that immigrants naturally, even unconsciously, fashion new cultural behaviours. Discussion of their identities should consider this hybridization, understand what it is, and determine whether there are enough social economic and social structures to make it viable.

The Viability of Ethnic Cultural Retention

We have pointed out so far that the cultures immigrants bring change considerably, and that their language develops reflections of such changes. In doing so, we have generalized the process. We will proceed with a further analysis with this understanding in mind.

As described above, appropriate social structures are necessary for a culture to be transmitted and shared among members of a particular ethnocultural group. If these social structures exist, along with other conditions of sociability, then the development and preservation of a distinct cultural identity is possible. It is only under such conditions that a culture can flourish through a living language and its related artistic expression. Our position is that this is not the case for Canada's ethnic cultures. There is an inadequate presence of ethnic, social, and economic structures to enable it. Ethnic categories with the potential to come together lack the necessary spatial cohesion to enable ethnic social structures to deal with their issues.

Without spatial cohesion, ethnic social structures cannot emerge to take care of scattered groups of ethnics. A major problem that ethnics face when they consider establishing social structures for themselves relates to the lack of a territorial base on which their institutions can be centred. Kogila Moodley comments on the effect of this for the establishment of ethnic schools: "Almost all Canadian schools are truly integrated ethnically. Indeed, the proportion of children from non-English-speaking homes sometimes exceeds fifty percent in metropolitan areas, although they do come from a vast variety of countries and cultures. While the former ethnic schools in the cultural ghetto could frequently cultivate mother tongue instructions albeit after school hours, the new multicultural environment puts a premium on the shedding of the original language."[8] Anderson notes a similar situation regarding the Ukrainian-Canadian school: "The small country schoolhouses in the bloc settlements have been replaced since the 1950s by large consolidated schools, many of which are in ethnically heterogonous centres, lessening the attention paid to consideration of ethnic origins."[9]

The issue of spatial dispersal is not related only to schools, but to the entire cohesion of ethnic categories and potential ethnic groups. As Anderson points out with respect to Ukrainians: "Largely gone are the intimate small communities upon which so many aspects of ethnic intra-group life were based."[10] This is not just the situation with Ukrainian-Canadians who have moved from rural areas to achieve better social position in other parts of Canada. It is difficult to think of any other group that functions primarily in one specific location. Chinese-Canadians, who at the beginning of this century suffered from racism and once lived in close-knit communities in certain areas of British Columbia, have since moved to other areas of Canada. Sociologist Graham E. Johnson reports that "in the 1970s the Chinese community is less confined geographically than it was in earlier periods of history. British Columbia still has the largest concentration of Chinese-Canadians, but that pre-eminence is challenged by Ontario. This is a reflection of the economic attraction of metropolitan Toronto for an immigrant population that seems upwardly mobile with new possibility of achieving career and other success."[11]

When we think of Italian-Canadians, similar dynamics apply. There are said to be close to one million people in Canada whose ancestry can be traced to Italy. That impressive number, though, does not consider that many of these people, despite their Italian ancestry, do not necessarily relate to an Italian-Canadian cultural ethnicity; nor does it take into account that they are scattered across Canada. Even in centres like Toronto, where a sizable portion of this population lives, they can be found from Etobicoke to Scarborough. This makes it difficult, even within metropolitan Toronto, to have a central location that could be a base for social structures catering to their cultural needs.

In such situations, what often happens is that even people of Italian or other ancestry who feel a distinctive ethnic identity, and who would like to live in keeping with that identity, are compelled to forgo this desire and begin to function in mainstream Canadian institutions. The cultural identity that they feel distinguishes them from others is acted out only in the confines of private relations or at special occasions when special effort is made to reach an Italian-Canadian institution.

We want to add another reflection here regarding spatial segregation. The move away from ethnically segregated neighbourhoods is not something ethnics necessarily deplore. In fact, it is typically the opposite. Most ethnics who at the beginning of their Canadian experience have had to live in inferior neighbourhoods see the move from these areas as a sign of their economic and social progress, especially when there has been considerable pressure to remain within certain areas of a city. Some of this was psychological, in the sense that immigrants were not made to feel welcome in some areas, and as soon as immigrants moved in, others began to move out — much like what happens in the U.S. with black and white people. Some forms of exclusion from particular areas of Canadian cities were at one time even enforced by local regulations. For example, in neighbourhoods of Hamilton, Ontario, restrictive covenants during the first half of the twentieth century prohibited the sale of homes to specified categories of immigrants.

It should surprise no one, then, that ethnics wanted to move beyond the confines that others had set out for them, whether officially or informally. Those who decry the spatial dispersal of ethnics fail to realize that whatever ethnic cohesion has existed has been induced by racists who want to keep their own neighbourhoods "pure" and confine the "undesirables" to their quarters. In apartheid South Africa, for example, strict laws exist to regulate ethnic boundaries, making it effectively a mosaic. The liberal nature of Canada does not permit it. The relative open-mindedness of some Canadians, combined with the desire and efforts of ethnics to get out of the "ghetto," has made it possible for ethnics to live anywhere they wish, according to their financial means.

Intermarriage is another factor influencing the viability of ethnic cultures. As more couples of mixed ethnic backgrounds marry, the participation in distinctive ethnic social structures will diminish. This is particularly true for the offspring of such marriages. American sociologist Herbert J. Gans poses these questions: "How would the son of an Italian mother and Irish father who has married a woman of Polish-German ancestry determine his ethnicity, and what would he and his wife tell their children [about their ethnicity]? Even if they were willing, would they be able to do so; and in that case to decide their children's ethnicity, how would they rank or synthetize their diverse backgrounds?"[12]

Intermarriage in Canada is common. Despite racism, prejudice, and the resistance of ethnic chauvinists, people in mixed workplaces and schools and participating in broad-based activities often find partners of differing ethnicity. Alberta sociologist Alexander Matejko reports that even as far back as 1961, intermarriages constituted two-thirds of all marriages for Polish males. For the Ukrainians, it was slightly more than half. He also points out that even among the Jewish population, intermarriages are rising.[13] John Porter points out that this is hardly reversible and that exogenous marriage due to urbanization and high levels of industrialization will continue to rise.[14]

This is not viewed positively by ideologists of the mosaic. Often, they appeal to the young to marry within their own ethnic groups. South Africa created laws specifically to prohibit intermarriage. Even in liberal Canadian society, we have people who, guided by a vision of the Canadian mosaic, encourage endogamy. As Porter puts it, "There was a time when lowering rates of endogamy could be taken as a sign of lessening prejudices, an indication that people of all groups would indeed allow their daughters or sisters to 'marry one [of them].' In the current view of the ideologists of the mosaic, the opposite is nurtured. For them it is better to exclude than to include. The metal of endogamy is more attractive because it is un-meltable."[15]

We have argued that intermarriage and spatial dispersal of potential ethnic groups erode opportunities for setting up appropriate social structures that could transmit ethnic cultures. Having these institutions is crucial for the social manifestations of different cultural behaviours. Their absence or limited presence confines ethnic cultural behaviours to being expressed only in the home or other limited settings. Cultures need social institutions to enable their members to live out their ethnic identities. They permit and facilitate the transmission of customs, traditions, and outlooks that will guide the individual member of a particular cultural group throughout his or her life. As Naomi R. White puts it, "The core of a culture is its system of institutions. By 'institutions' is meant that complex of social relationships which serve to organize childrearing, worship, labour and leisure."[16] "An institution," she adds, "is any fixed mode of thought or behaviour held by a group of individuals which can be communicated and generally accepted, and the violation of which causes a disturbance."[17]

In this sense, when we speak of ethnic social institutions, we do not mean only ethnic halls, cafés, or restaurants, which allow ethnics to go out occasionally to express their ethnicity. To flourish, ethnic groups need access to their own schools, places of worship, and specific political organizations. In short, they need the same institutions that mainstream society has at its disposal. As we have already pointed out, the days of Canadian ethnic schools are gone. These were only very few to begin with and existed mainly in rural western Canada. Perhaps it was with this in mind that some people of the Ukrainian-Canadian and Armenian-Canadian communities in Toronto proposed that the Toronto Board of Education create alternative-language schools that would exclude pupils of other backgrounds. The proposal was not accepted and, perhaps due to this refusal, these forces, along with members of other ethnic communities, introduced a proposal for third-language instruction. Let us leave this discussion for later, when we will analyze it more fully. For now, let us just say that in Canada, the education of the young does not take place in segregated ethnic schools or classrooms.

Similarly, participation in the Canadian political process does not take place along ethnic lines. The political activities of hyphenated Canadians take place within established local-riding associations. Although the composition of these may in some areas reflect a higher presence of one particular ethnic group, they do not exclude others from participating. Here again we have to draw a distinction between an organization that is created for an ethnic group and one that welcomes all. If political cultural pluralism existed in Canada, all the major parties would have corresponding ethnic organizations and elect ethnic politicians to speak on behalf of their ethnic groups. This is not the case. There are different groupings within all major Canadian parties and in government and they come together not on the question of ethnicity, but in relation to other economic and political imperatives.

We have looked at some social institutions that we feel are essential for projecting and transmitting an ethnocultural identity. The list is certainly not complete. Still, we think we have made the point that the cultures immigrants bring, and which eventually develop into hybrid ones, do not have the appropriate social structures to be sustained. Even the cultural identities of large ethnocultural groups served by substantial social structures are in jeopardy. Anderson comments on this in relation to Ukrainian-Canadians. Although he acknowledges that a sort of institutional completeness and strong ethnic self-awareness did exist in the past, he points out that there are many indications that this ethnic self-awareness is likely to continue to decrease in all possibility at an accelerated rate.[18] Matejko indicates a similar situation with Polish-Canadians. He states, "Poles in Canada today constitute a conglomerate of various local groups in limited touch with one another. A very substantial part of the more than 300,000 people of Polish origin have no contact with the Polish-Canadian ethnic institutions."[19]

Moving from observations about these ethnic groups to a more general one, we'd like to conclude with the words of sociologists Lance W. Roberts and R.A. Clifton: "In fact, very few Canadian groups have social structures that can effectively restrict their members should they choose to follow the lures of non-traditional ways of life. Without the organizational capacity to govern interactions in these ways, uncontrolled changes become probable and an ethnic group's capacity to perpetuate its cultural heritage decreases."[20]

Symbolic Ethnicity

We have described the process of acculturation that transforms the original culture of immigrants to a hybrid culture. We have further indicated that factors such as inter-ethnic marriages and the lack of specific territorial bases erode these cultural identities as potential ethnic aggregates begin to participate in mainstream cultural institutions. Once the process of acculturation begins, it is difficult to imagine this process will be reversed. Reversing acculturation would require various levels of government to adopt policies that would induce potential members of ethnocultural groups to find suitable socio-economic opportunities within their groups, to seek marriage partners within their own groups, and to establish more definitive territorial boundaries in which ethnics could function socially and culturally. In other words, it would require making Canada effectively a mosaic. If this is not done — and we assume that it will not, considering the liberal democratic traditions of Canadian society — the process of acculturation will not stop. With acculturation, behavioural remnants of ethnicities would still be present in Canadian society but would become merely symbolic. Let us explain.

In the absence of appropriate social structures, a new type of ethnicity emerges, which hinges more on symbols of the past than practised cultural behaviour. When acculturation transforms an ethnicity, that ethnicity is expressed differently. As Gans puts it, "A new kind of ethnic involvement may be occurring, which emphasizes concerns with identity, with the feelings of being Jewish or Italian, etc. Since ethnic identity needs are neither intense nor frequent in this generation, ethnics do not need either ethnic cultures or organizations; instead, they resort to the rise of ethnic symbols."[21] It essentially boils down to some symbols of an ethnic culture becoming visible and expressed within mainstream society.

The forms that such symbolic ethnicity can take are innumerable. However, what essentially distinguishes them from earlier cultural expressions is that the ethnic identity of the people who manifest them is not anchored to organized groups. Instead, they find their identity by affiliating with an abstract collectivity. For these people, the ethnocultural traditions of the first generation are not important to their everyday lives. They are more comfortable expressing their identities in intermittent ways that do not conflict with the new roles they have assumed in society. In this situation, ethnic identity takes on a different meaning. While in the past it had derived from a lived cultural difference, albeit partial, the new identity is merely a perceived difference, stemming from the awareness of an ethnic ancestry. The ethnocultural behaviour of old is no longer integral to their being. Instead, certain symbols are taken from that behaviour to express the new ethnic identity. Gans summarizes it in this way: "In other words, as the functions of ethnic cultures and groups diminish ... ethnicity takes on an expressive rather than institutional function in people's lives, becoming more of a leisure-time activity and losing its relevance, say, to earning a living or regulating family life."[22]

Reflecting on the Canadian ethnic situation, we cannot say ethnics in Canada today express only a symbolic identity. Although ethnics do not have appropriate social structures to fully transmit their cultural behaviour, and although interest in a type of ethnicity that is rooted in ethnic social structures is waning, we do have ethnics who display distinct cultural behaviour. However, the process of acculturation continues, compelling people who still feel an attachment to their ethnic origins to display them in a symbolic way. The culture of their immigrant parents or grandparents becomes something of the past, to which their allegiance is only emblematic. As Gans states, "Cultures which the immigrants brought with them are now only an ancestral memory, or an exotic tradition to be savoured once in a while in a museum or at an ethnic festival."[23] This "is characterized by a nostalgic allegiance to the culture of the immigrant generation, or that of the old country; a love for and a pride in a tradition that can be felt without having to be incorporated in everyday behaviour."[24]

This process we are describing is reflected in the language used by immigrants and their offspring. Again, if we make the assumption that a language is integral to a culture and that changes in one will reflect changes in the other, language will act as a measure of the degree to which ethnics have assumed symbolic ethnic identities.

We have explained before how acculturation affects the language immigrants bring over. These changes begin to take place from the very beginning, so that in a matter of weeks, the Italian immigrant, for example, will begin to use the word *fattoria* for factory instead of *fabbrica*. But even this hybrid language, which is integral to the cultural behaviour of ethnics, becomes in time a relic of the past for the second generation and those following. Matejko points out, "Language ceases to be an important basis of social differentiation in the second and subsequent generations."[25] Anderson indicates the same for Ukrainian-Canadians, and Statistics Canada reports that virtually all Scandinavians speak English at home, and that 80 to 90 percent of Dutch, Germans, and Finns do likewise. Only one-fifth of Slavs use their native language in the home.[26]

Certainly, the language of second- and third-generation ethnics is English, and they typically lack a knowledge of either the standard or hybrid language of their ancestors. However, at the appropriate time, those who still have an ethnic "feeling" may throw in a word from these languages. It is not unusual to hear a young Italian-Canadian whose identity has been formed in the Canadian context use greetings like *ciao* or *come stai* and then proceed to converse only in English. Their knowledge of Italian may not extend much beyond that, but by using such words, they are indicating a need to identify with their ancestors' culture. The language of their ancestors becomes only a taste to savour once in a while.

A good example of this symbolic identity is the case of the Scots in Canada. As anthropologist Judith A. Nagata points out, "Scottish-Canadians can be considered as little more than a diffuse category (but by no means a group) of individuals who acknowledge an ultimate common origin and a vague sense of identity. Aside from the occasional burst of cultural revitalization in the form of such rather self-conscious activities as the Highland Games, the Canadian Scots have a low social and cultural profile, and no demonstrable claim to be a true community, in the strict sense of the word."[27] The Scots in Canada may sport the bagpipes or the kilt, or give English words a brogue intonation when they want to indicate a pride with their past. However, the language they use is not Gaelic but English, and when the festivities are over, they shed their kilts.

In this respect, the recent amiable "Shamrock Summit" between Prime Minister Brian Mulroney and President Ronald Reagan provides a fine example of symbolic ethnicity. What other significance could we give to these two political leaders making homage to their Irish ancestry? If we take these references as genuine — that is, not made for political considerations but as a sincerely felt allegiance to their ancestry — we can only conclude that they feel pride in their ancestors and regard themselves as symbols of that group. It is doubtful they are part of organized Irish-Canadian and Irish-American groups, and it is self-evident they display cultural attributes that would identify them as mainstream Canadians and mainstream Americans, and not as Irish people of Ireland.

Ethnic Artistic Expressions

We have indicated in the preceding pages a process that transforms the original cultures of immigrants to hybrid cultures and then to symbolic cultures. We have also seen how language reflects these changes. We understand that a language is an expression of a culture, and that a culture, to sustain itself, needs to develop and cherish it. Language and culture work symbiotically to maintain one another. Art, in general, reflects that relationship. As a result, there should be a process of acculturation in artistic expression similar to the one we see in language. If this does not happen, then we can either say there is no ethnic cultural distinction or, if we still maintain that ethnocultural differences can be witnessed in Canada, that there must be a number of social and cultural factors that do not allow these differences to be expressed artistically.

Our position stands with the second hypothesis. Under appropriate circumstances, the popular manifestations of a distinct cultural behaviour should yield some form of artistic expression anchored in this distinction. This is not the case. Some expressions do occur: immigrants have expressed in poetry, music, painting, and other forms of art their experience as immigrants and their visions of life filtered through their newly acquired cultural behaviour. But such expression has not been enough to permit immigrants and members of particular ethnocultural groups to fully reflect their lives. In other words, artistic expressions have not corresponded in quantity, and perhaps quality, to the popular ethnocultural manifestations.

This is owing to a number of reasons, primarily the economic situation in which most first-generation ethnics find themselves. Generally speaking, a solid economic base is needed to support artistic creativity. Furthermore, on their arrival to Canada, most immigrants are faced with two problems that impede their artistic creativity. First, they need to devote all their energies to immediate necessities. Immigrants usually do not come with capital sufficient to give them social and economic security. Consequently, they direct their efforts almost exclusively to securing enough material wealth to provide a sense of economic security. They typically have to take on demanding jobs, leaving little room to express artistic creativity or even to appreciate it. It's also important to note that most people who have emigrated for economic reasons have little formal education and also lack the artistic skills or training needed to project their vision of life as lived in their new social setting. It is not unusual to hear immigrants express frustration over not being able to share with others what they experience, and lamenting the lack of skills to do so.

Another contributor to the scarcity of immigrants' ethnic artistic expression, apart from their own precarious economic status, is the lack of financial support for artistic creativity within their own community and society at large. There is typically little financial return for publishers to invest in immigrants' cultural products. Further, there is not sufficient economic interest to sustain an ethnic view beneficial to the ethnic community itself. The economic activities and interests of an ethnic community are typically not large enough to generate a corresponding investment in artistic expression, including expensive advertising.

This does not mean there is no interest from ethnic businesses or organizations that could benefit from ethnic artistic expression. However, these are usually too small and lack the economic power to take on the burden of promoting the arts. Often their potential for survival and growth requires making inroads into other communities. Ironically, this would demand shedding their ethnic coats, as the promotion of a distinct ethnocultural expression could be detrimental to their economic welfare. In summary, the lifestyles of recent immigrants and those more rooted in Canadian society — the hybrid ones — do not find ethnic artistic expression and exposure to the public to be sustainable.

The federal government's policy of multiculturalism is meant to overcome these problems. It intends to provide financial assistance to ethnocultural groups and to generate an interest in the cultural expression of ethnic identities. Unfortunately, this intention is not well realized. First, the policy, in practice, lends more assistance to ethnic cultural expression via the English language. Second, financial support, although theoretically free from political considerations, usually has political strings attached. Third, the people who typically take advantage of such policies are artists of the second and third generations who still feel some sort of allegiance to their ethnic roots.

There are a couple of additional points that need to be considered. The first relates to non-verbal artistic expression and the second to art forms that involve verbal communication.

The lack of financial backing and the absence of cultural structures hamper genuine and pertinent ethnic cultural expression. Not incidentally, this is more evident in the various forms of spoken artistic expression — for example, ethnic Canadians who seek to enter theatre or cinema and can speak English are more likely to choose to act in productions that target wider Canadian audiences. Opportunities in theatre within the ethnic community are very limited, as there is a lack of cultural and economic structures to sustain them. In addition, if our hypothetical actors choose to portray the cultural behaviour of a particular ethnic group, whatever their talent may be, they are likely to toil in obscurity unless they can put themselves before larger audiences.

The case is slightly different for the written arts. It is significant that when we think about ethnic artists, what typically comes to mind are poets and novelists. Writing is the one field where ethnocultural expression is flourishing. Whether it is Irving Layton writing about his Jewish roots, Mary di Michele's very poignant and poetic reflections on her Italian-Canadian experiences, or Vera Lysenko discussing her Ukrainian-Canadian background, we may say ethnic literature is coming of age. The problem, however, with this literature is that it is not made for the consumption of the ethnic population. Apart from its enjoyment by mainstream Canadians, it is only symbolic ethnics who see reflections of themselves and make use of it. This literature is presented almost exclusively in English and, as with other forms of artistic expression, it does not find the appropriate outlets to reach immigrants who arrived earlier.

The use of English, and not the original languages of immigrants, or the hybrid versions of those languages, is significant in itself. It is not necessarily the case of a writer preferring one language over another, but the idea that English, in most cases, is the only tool they have to properly express their feelings and ideas. Certainly enough, the odd Yiddish, Italian, or Ukrainian word makes the ethnicity of the writer more evident, but such reminders are more indicative of where the artist has come from, not of where they are now. This is not unlike the symbolic ethnic identity of people of second and subsequent generations who occasionally use an ethnic word or symbol to show affection for and pride in their origin, but who on an everyday basis do not socially behave as distinguishable ethnics.

The content of such literature also has a symbolic nature. Generally, it does not describe ethnic matters from within a group but from the outside. The vantage point is of the person who has gone through it, not one who is still in it. The literature of these ethnic writers describes what life in the ethnic community was like for them as they were growing up, or as they remember others speaking of it, but not what it is like in the present. Whether this is done from a sense of nostalgia — remembering close-knit neighbourhoods and the fragrances of shops and homes — or to lament what they have had to endure, the point is that almost invariably, it is an act of looking back at the world as it was. It is the recollection of people who no longer participate in ethnic activities or who never did, except perhaps occasionally, and who are not involved in ethnic organizations. As their ethnic identity is symbolic so, in a sense, is their literary work.

This is not a criticism of their literature, nor of their symbolic ethnic identity. It is simply an acknowledgement. These writers express views and feelings about life from where they are. They cannot do otherwise. They are undergoing a process of acculturation but have not been assimilated to the point that they reject their past. On the contrary, they proudly display signs of their ethnic origins. If we consider this a new form of ethnic identity, or another stage in the process of acculturation, we may say they also live it. Their literature is a genuine reflection of this newly felt form of ethnicity. The demands these artists would or could make on mainstream Canadian society are different from those of ethnics from earlier generations. Still, this is a question we will deal with later when we present an alternative to the vision of the Canadian mosaic. For now, let us see how the ideologists of the mosaic confront this situation.

Imported Culture

The position of ideologists of the mosaic is that the cultures of immigrants and their descendants are durable and persistent, despite altered social, economic, and political conditions. We constantly hear them speak of Canada's cultural mosaic and the vibrant cultures within each piece of the mosaic. They point out that ethnics (non-French and non-English) represent one-third of Canada's population and, as such, should have every right to speak in their "own" languages and project their "own" culture. However, an interesting phenomenon occurs in the passage from words to actions and the need to set up cultural and language programs for an ethnic group or ethnic aggregation. It is in this phase, putting their ideology into practice, where they encounter problems. They do not have at their disposal cultural products to offer to the intended ethnic users. The life that ethnic groups live is not well reflected in the news media, the theatres, or other cultural institutions. As described above, it is not represented in the ethnic artistic world; nor is it apparent in the artistic expression of the mainstream.

Facing this situation and lacking sufficient room to promote cultural creativity within an ethnic group, cultural entrepreneurs go back to the immigrant's country of origin for their programs. One has only to look at what is offered on television programs, in theatres, and on radio stations that cater to ethnic communities to understand what "ethnic" cultural product is offered. Almost universally it comes from abroad and uses the standard languages of the countries from which it is imported. Modern technological developments such as satellites have made this even more possible. For example, cable television, via satellite, has lately been offering programs directly from Italy on a daily basis. Greek-Canadians, Spanish-speaking Canadians, German-Canadians, and almost all others can access similar material from their ancestral countries. In this way, ethnic groups are culturally dependent on what their former countries are willing and able to offer. These programs add another dimension of alienation. Their viewers' lives unfold in a Canadian setting, while what is offered does not reflect their new way of life.

An essential characteristic of culture is its ability to bind people together and offer solace in times of distress. This comfort is hardly available to immigrants. Their hybrid ethnic lives are not reflected in what they see or read, and what is available for them through the mainstream media is not relevant. Even when they are quite knowledgeable about their former countries and have definite ideas on what they would do if they were there, the fact remains that ethnics living in Canada are not "back home." They are not able to participate in the socio-political activities of those countries. Even when they join groups that promote some sort of political and social stance in regard to what is happening there, like Polish-Canadians supporting the Solidarity movement in Poland, the impact they can achieve is so minimal that they feel powerless and frustrated. In addition, these activities are marginal to their lives in Canada. It is a twilight existence: they are alienated from here and from there.

There may be no better example of this than the Italian-Canadian population and the 1982 World Cup soccer championship. As the Italian team progressed through the final rounds and ultimately became champions, hundreds of thousands of Italian-Canadians poured into the streets of Toronto and other Canadian cities to celebrate. In the midst of their joy, a sense of sorrow was also present. The games of this soccer championship, as with other events concerning Italy, although exciting, could be experienced by Italian-Canadians only via satellite. This was the basis of the expressed sadness: the sorrow of a life lived via satellite.

The gap between what ethnic Canadians need and what is offered to them culturally is starkly evident in the language programs provided to ethnic children. We have seen that the languages ethnics speak in the home are really hybrid versions. This is especially so for the second generation, which either communicates exclusively in English or uses a hybrid language in the home. Language-instruction programs on offer do not reflect this. They use the standard versions of their immigrant parents' or grandparents' languages. The problem with this is that they are made to feel obliged to learn them in these original forms because they are told these are their languages and they have a duty to learn them "properly." The ethnic media and some ethnic organizations and activists perpetuate this message. The reality, of course, is different. The non-English language that they speak, if they speak one at all, is a hybrid, so students react negatively to language programs that have little bearing on their lives. The standard language used does not express the experience of the ethnic child, just as the cultural programs that come from abroad are removed from the ethnic group's daily cultural life.

Chapter 9

Canadian Mainstream Culture

To debate whether there is a mainstream culture in Canada could be considered a waste of time, yet it has to be done because the denial of a cultural mainstream is central to the position of the ideologists of the mosaic. It is reasonable to assume that as people came to Canada, whether as settlers or immigrants, they all had to adjust to a particular set of conditions. The Canadian climate itself, the relationships between cultural groups, and the types of economic activities they had to undertake to survive all demanded that people live differently than they had in their previous countries. Freezing them in the cultures of their past was simply not possible. Regardless of where they came from, they had to adjust. In the process, a distinct Canadian lifestyle developed, which is not like the British or the French or the German way of life, but uniquely Canadian.

American sociologist Milton Yinger, reflecting on this aspect of the U.S., concludes that the culture there "is not simply an off-shoot of British or British and North European culture or even British and European culture generally, to which other groups have been to a greater or lesser degree cultured in a one-way process. The total culture contains values, objects, art, technologies, and other cultural items drawn from the whole range of people who make up American society."[1]

The ideologists of the mosaic, by not considering in their analysis and vision the existence of a cultural mainstream, deny that different cultures establish relationships with each other and, in the process, change. It is true that ethnic cultures exist, but as George Bancroft, a University of Toronto professor of West Indian background, has pointed out, multiculturalism should mean something other than the notion of a Canadian mosaic.

> When we talk about the multicultural society in Canada, we talk of the culturally pluralistic society in which that which forms the common core or cement is no longer merely Anglo-Saxon or Gallic, valuable though these have been in the past, but something called "Canadian" produced from the womb of a land whose sweep Morley Callaghan terms "majestic." We have a land of dreams, fostered by an "atmosphere" that recognizes that while a historic debt is owed to the Indian, French and British, what now exists, this current common core — is not a pale imitation of these, but a new growth to which the term "Canadian" applies.[2]

We would agree and affirm that a Canadian cultural mainstream has developed from the interaction between different cultural traditions. Still, we want to make a couple of observations, first by reflecting on the barriers that some cultural behaviours have encountered to becoming part of the mainstream, and second, by pointing out the dominant role that British culture has had in this respect.

Canadian society has displayed a significant degree of resistance to accepting the lifestyles of immigrant groups as they have entered and established themselves in their new country. For instance, in the immediate post–Second World War period and into the early 1950s, people who wanted to play soccer encountered enormous difficulties. The game was not considered Canadian and people who wanted to play it often heard they "should pack their bags and go home." Although there were no legal restrictions banning them from playing the game, there were no fields or nets available, and no one in authority cared to make them a priority. It was only through the persistence of immigrant groups, including the newer waves of British newcomers, that the game made inroads into Canadian society. Now Canada has a national soccer team and there are professional soccer teams in several Canadian cities. Even more important, soccer is commonly played by schoolchildren — and not just the ethnic ones.

That said, we are hardly suggesting that rigidity toward newcomers' cultural traditions is something of the past. Established Canadian cultural institutions and the media do very little to correct this situation. While more people besides the immigrant children play soccer, more people besides the Germans celebrate Oktoberfest, more people beyond the Italians eat pasta, more people than just the Poles dance to polka tunes, and more people besides the Irish celebrate St. Patrick's Day, the media still label these activities "ethnic." The example of soccer proves this point. Although the popularity of this sport now reaches well beyond a handful of ethnic groups, the media, with some rare exceptions, rarely discuss it. The net effect of this lack of public openness toward other cultural behaviours delays the entry of new cultural traditions into the mainstream to become the patrimony of all.

It seems immigrant cultural groups are able to inject elements of their cultures into the mainstream only once they have endured a substantial amount of discrimination and harassment. This phenomenon is well illustrated by the case of the Irish. Today, Prime

Minister Brian Mulroney can proudly and publicly lay claim to his Irish ancestry, and on St. Patrick's Day, even the beer in Canada's bars is coloured green. In the past, though, as A.E. Ryerson wrote in 1858, the Irish were considered "the precursors of the worse pestilence of social insubordination and disorder."[3]

Another observation that can be made when looking at the Canadian cultural mainstream is that not all have contributed equally to it. To believe so would be wishful thinking. The continuous connection between Canada and England has permitted people of British origin to have an unequal influence on the Canadian cultural tradition. This is not only in relation to the cultural behavioural patterns of the Canadian mainstream but also in its fundamental guiding values.

If we return to the distinction we have made previously about culture, in which we have a value component and a behavioural one, we will note that in the creation of Canada's value system, the British connection has held fundamental importance. We need only look at our parliamentary form of government, modelled directly on Westminster, to find the British matrix. The same is true of our legal system. Although it is based on the needs of Canadian society, it takes its values, nomenclature, and rules from the British legal system. The examples we could name are many, but the point is there is a direct relationship between Canada's fundamental values and Britain's.

This same influence must also be recognized in the cultural behaviour of Canada's mainstream population. If more than 43 percent of Canada's population is of British origin, it is difficult to imagine how this group would not have had the dominant impact it has had. The influence, of course, goes beyond population statistics. The impact of our colonial connection to England — in terms of political exchange, commodity trading, and open lines of communication — either did not exist in the same way for other groups of people and their former countries, or it was pared to an essential minimum. Essentially, we may conclude that for obvious reasons, the British have been culturally dominant in Canada.

The question here is not whether the basis, the essence, of the Canadian mainstream culture is British. It is whether Canadian culture is only of the British and for the British, or whether it belongs to or could belong to all. In a previous section, we stated that it is important to distinguish institutions that are exclusively of one's ethnic group from those in which a particular ethnicity might predominate, while still catering to all. The same needs to be done in regard to culture. If we can conclude that Canadian mainstream culture is and will never be anything but a culture transported from Britain, it would be clear that all Canadians of other cultural backgrounds should direct themselves to finding their appropriate cultural niches. If this is not the case, our efforts should be directed toward exploring venues that welcome an injection of immigrant cultural traits into the mainstream culture.

Artistic Expression of the Mainstream Culture

We have stated earlier that if a cultural behaviour exists, it will ultimately lead to its own artistic expression. Let us reflect on this in the context of the culture of the Canadian mainstream. Before that, though, let us make a distinction between what is usually referred to as the popular culture and what, at times, is called the "grand" or "high" culture of a people. This distinction is usually made between the customs, traditions, cuisine, sports, and pastimes of a people, or its lived culture, and its so-called high culture: music, literature, visual arts, and dance. In our minds, these two aspects of culture are inseparable, in the sense that artistic expressions emanate from popular cultural behaviour. High culture distills the cultural experiences of a people and reflects artists' understanding of their society. In turn, art becomes a medium to help people — through either direct or indirect messages — to understand themselves and their society.

Still, art cannot be viewed strictly as an instrument of a particular society and only that society. In fact, it is argued that when its creators and audiences are confined, art cannot flourish. Art should have universal significance. It should say something not only about the culture from which it springs, but also about society in general. In other words, it should confront or reflect the human condition, transcending restrictions of time and space. When we read Shakespeare or Dante or Tolstoy, we get more than a view of Elizabethan England, pre-Renaissance Italy, or czarist Russia. In the works of these writers and other artists like them, we can all see reflections of ourselves. Contemporary artists who deal with our present social problems would not be any different. If we look at the work of author Gabriel Garcia Marquez, for example, not only do we witness the writer's view of Colombian society, but those who live in other conditions can also see aspects of themselves and reflect on their own situations. Enduring works of art transcend the immediate experiences of their societies and speak about universal themes to which people living in other places and times can relate.

Returning to our Canadian concerns, if our assumption is correct that our country has a mainstream culture, we should be able to see it represented in art. Our position, contrary to that of the ideologists of the mosaic, is that genuinely Canadian artistic expression exists, emanating from a uniquely Canadian way of life. We need only consider some artists to prove our point.

Perhaps the most apparent expression of a uniquely Canadian way of life is in literature. The writing of Margaret Laurence, Margaret Atwood, and Farley Mowat do this for us. Whether it is preoccupation with rural life in western Canada, urban life in Toronto, or life in the barrens of northern Canada, these authors express views that expose and reflect on uniquely Canadian circumstances. They speak of a Canada and a Canadian lifestyle that is not associated with any particular ethnicity.

We need only look at "The Loons," a short story by Margaret Laurence, to understand that the story she is telling takes place not in the context of London, New York, or rural Scotland, but in a small Manitoban town. The loons she writes about, the mentality of people in a small town, and the ecological problems people face characterize specifically Canadian conditions.

In other forms of artistic expression, although they may not be as prolific, the essence of Canada provides a central theme. How else could we explain the preoccupation of painters such as the Group of Seven? It is true that in some ways their artistic techniques reflect foreign influences, but the content is purely Canadian. Their landscapes reflect the beauty of autumn, the harshness of winter, and the majesty of our forests, and serve to illustrate a Canadian attitude toward nature. Certainly, we cannot discredit such artistic expression as being less than authentically Canadian merely on the basis of style and technique. If these were the only basis for our judgment, they would probably lead us to disclaim many other recognized national artistic expressions. What would we say about Chaucer's *Canterbury Tales*? Would we say it is not part of England's literary expression because he based his tales on the Italian model of Boccaccio's *Decameron*?

Cinema provides another avenue for expressing Canadian culture. Although Canadian movies are not produced in the quantity or quality we would like, lately a good number of respectable films depicting Canadian life have been produced. The National Film Board has done this through documentaries, which have received international acclaim, and individual filmmakers have won recognition with dramatic movies dealing with themes that reflect life in this country.

However, the issue with Canadian culture is not that artistic expression does not exist, nor that the behaviour of Canadians does not allow for its development. The problem is that it has not been able to find adequate international recognition. Perhaps this is because Canadian artistic expression has lacked universal appeal. Still, the 1981 nomination of Irving Layton for a Nobel Prize confirms the international validity of Canadian literature and suggests that wider recognition is growing.

Unfortunately, Canadian culture and its corresponding artistic expression have suffered considerably because of Canada's colonial past with England and the present state of dependency on the U.S. This is not to say that a uniquely Canadian culture has not emerged, despite the roadblocks it has encountered, but that its artistic expression has been pushed to the background and its importance downplayed for Canadians and for others.

The idea of Canadian culture suffering because of close ties with England and the U.S. should not surprise anyone. The cultures of other countries that have experienced similar states of colonial dependence have been similarly stunted. Early American culture suffered in the same way. Only in this century has the U.S. been able to shed the condescension of England, which once controlled its economic and political life. The same is true of many Latin American cultures that were looked down upon by the Spanish conquerors, who felt that cultural expressions from their colonies were not on par with their own.

Such examples indicate a particular kind of cultural relationship between a "mother" country and a dependent one. The idea behind this kind of relationship is simple: if people can be convinced that they do not have a culture of their own, or if their cultural expression can be shown to be inferior, it will be easier for others to thwart the economic and political ambitions of a dependent country. Cultural affirmation goes hand in hand with political and economic independence. The inverse is also true: political and economic domination also demands corresponding hegemony in the realm of culture. The forms this may take are numerous and include directly crushing a dependent country's culture or starving it slowly by blocking its connection to the appropriate markets for it.

Canada falls into the latter circumstance. Canadian art in general has not only lacked the opportunity to be distributed beyond its borders but has also been kept from reaching its first and most natural audience: Canadians. Canada's cultural structures, whether they be publishing houses, art galleries, or outlets for film distribution, resort to promoting works by Canadian artists only when other foreign cultural products are not available. The rationale, even if at times it is not stated, is that Canadian art is inferior to that which comes from Europe or the U.S.

Educational institutions, which help determine the essence of any nation, have also lacked in this regard. Until recently, Canadian high schools did not feature Canadian short stories, novels, or poems in their courses. The situation was similar in Canadian universities. A student majoring in literature could graduate without taking any courses in Canadian literature. Students would be required to study British literature, from *Beowulf* to D.H. Lawrence, and be expected to take a number of courses in American literature, but none in Canadian literature.

The situation has recently changed substantially, particularly since the second half of the 1970s. Courses in Canadian literature are now mandatory in most Canadian university English programs, and in high schools, Canadian writers are now featured in the literature curriculum.

Improved exposure to Canadian literature and film has not happened accidentally. It is the result of pressure Canadians have exerted on their governments, asking for their cultural needs to be met. This does not mean Canadian cultural life and the artistic expression of that life have entered safe waters. On the contrary: although the English colonial past no longer presents a significant barrier to independent national artistic expression, American cultural influence is a lingering and growing threat. The wide distribution of films in the Canadian market, the pervasive presence of American television, the flooding of our libraries and bookstores with American books, and the looming presence of American businesses selling American cultural products suggest the development of Canadian artistic expression will continue to be challenging. What has emerged and cannot be underestimated is an awareness that a Canadian cultural identity does exist, and as such needs to be expressed artistically and shared through robust channels of distribution. These demands for the genuine artistic expression of the Canadian cultural identity go hand in hand with workers demanding independent Canadian unions, the effort to build an independent national economy, and demands that Canadians should set the course of their political action based on what they consider best for themselves.

These views, considerations, and interests do not align with the ideology of the mosaic. By focusing on the Canadian cultural mosaic, its adherents deny — in theory and in practice — the existence of a Canadian cultural mainstream whose identity is specifically and uniquely Canadian. Their demands threaten to fragment Canadian society culturally and politically.

Our efforts in this section have been directed to proving that a Canadian culture exists and distinguishes Canadians from people of other nationalities. We have called this a "mainstream Canadian culture" as it reflects the cultural behaviour of those people who do not see themselves as ethnics and who function within Canadian institutions that do not belong to any particular ethnicity. We have also tried to show that this Canadian cultural behaviour finds expression through corresponding forms of art, despite the fact that Canada's cultural development has been hampered by our colonial past with England and our proximity to the U.S.

Chapter 10

The Adverse Effects of the Ideology of the Mosaic

The ideology of the mosaic is a construct composed of some significant and fundamental assumptions that are not correct. The validity of an ideology cannot be based only on what it claims. Instead, we need to look at its assumptions, which determine and shape its socio-political objectives. An ideology is a motive force that leads its proponents to interpret reality in a certain way, and then channels social demands along its vision of society. What determines the direction and the eventual results of some policies is not their stated objectives but the assumptions of the ideology that act as an undercurrent. Operating on false assumptions, policies stemming from the ideology of the mosaic, which set political programs and initiatives regarding the integration of ethnics into Canadian society, do not and cannot provide the expected and intended results. In fact, we witness a disjunction between stated objectives and results.

With the application of policies stemming from the ideology of the cultural mosaic, the various disjunctions between stated objective and actual non-corresponding results have been generally overlooked. Sectors of the Canadian social fabric — such as Native political leaders, Quebecois politicians and other French-speaking

Canadians, the Acadians, and mainstream Canadians — do not see themselves as part of specific ethnic groups and oppose being relegated to just "ethnics." This disjunction or contradiction becomes more evident with the partial implementation of the third-language policy of the Toronto Board of Education, a policy strongly promoted by ideologists of the mosaic. Let us examine what consequences the vision of the mosaic may have, both for those outside of ethnic groups and for ethnics themselves.

The response of the Quebecois to the vision of the mosaic has been almost unanimously negative. These people have not reacted this way out of bigotry or resistance to newcomers practising their own cultural heritage. On the contrary, they have understood clearly that ethnic groups have cultural aspirations which a democratic society cannot deny them. As Claude Ryan points out, "I straight away endorse any government policy aimed at granting reasonable financial assistance to volunteer groups, free institutions which stem from the will of the ethnic or cultural groups which wish to continue to manifest themselves according to their own merit."[1] Having said that, Ryan goes on to illustrate his reasons for rejecting the policy of multiculturalism. What he and the Quebecois oppose is an interpretation of this policy that equates the needs and aspirations of ethnic groups to the aspirations of Quebec. As we have stated, the policy of multiculturalism is ambiguous, permitting different visions to be formulated around its tenets, of which the mosaic is the most insidious. Quebecois in particular have responded negatively, not to the aspirations of ethnics but to the vision that Canada is a mosaic of which they form one piece, just like any other ethnic group. They have insisted instead that for social and historical reasons, the Quebecois are different and their rights and demands go beyond those of ethnic groups. Ideologists of the mosaic, by insisting on their vision of Canada, deny them such recognition.

The idealism behind these objectives seems appealing but is based on a false assumption that diminishes the political will of the Quebecois. As we have pointed out before, the Quebecois have the attributes to be considered a national ethnic group. Whether it is ultimately possible for them to set up their own nation, or whether it is desirable to remain as they are, are not the questions we set out to deal with here. However, we must recognize that the differences between the Quebecois and ethnic groups do not permit allegiances regarding common demands regarding ethnicity. Giving similar status to the two would essentially mean diminishing the aspirations of the Quebecois. The policy of multiculturalism, when viewed from a mosaic perspective, proves this point. It should not come as a surprise to have Quebecois from different walks of life and politicians of different parties claim special status for Quebec and oppose a vision that allows them only the same rights as ethnic groups.

Canada's Native population and French-Canadians outside Quebec are in similar situations and oppose the policy for similar reasons. Native Canadians, again for historical and social reasons, do not find common ground with ethnic groups. They view themselves as distinct, with cultural, political, and territorial demands that have no connection to ethnic groups' demands. It should not be surprising, then, to find a lack of collaboration among these sets of people.

Similarly, French-Canadians outside Quebec, especially Acadians, draw distinctions between themselves and ethnics. Representatives of the Fédération acadienne de la Nouvelle-Écosse were clear that they consider multiculturalism unhelpful in their community's linguistic and cultural development. Seeing as French is one of the founding cultures of Canada, they held that their linguistic rights would not be guaranteed under a multicultural policy. The group officially rejected multiculturalism in October 1973.

Mainstream Canadians also reject this policy as viewed from the position of the mosaic ideology. They reject the notion that all Canadians need to be hyphenated and they resist attempts by the ideologists of the mosaic to slot them into ethnic categories. Unlike the character of the young schoolgirl in the musical play we described earlier, they do not see any ethnic problem for themselves and happily continue to behave socially in their non-ethnic context.

We have tried to point out broadly that the ideology of the mosaic is an imposition on many groups and that the policy of multiculturalism, when interpreted from this perspective, is opposed by social forces that do not see their interests represented fairly. Emblematically, the third-language instruction policy passed by the Toronto Board of Education represents the summation of several incorrect assumptions regarding ethnicity in Canada. These erroneous assumptions give rise to heated disputes and conflicts. Although certain forces within ethnic groups are in favour of the policy and push for it, others foresee negative consequences and oppose its full implementation. We will spend considerable time discussing the various aspects of this policy to determine its validity for ethnic school children.

The policy of third-language instruction is based on the pedagogical concept that children learn and feel better if they receive instruction in their own language. This is unquestionably true. People in general feel better, work more productively, and learn more in their own language while interacting within their own cultural traditions. What has to be questioned here is not the educational concept, but the imposition of this theory as it relates to Canadian ethnic children, especially its social implications. The policy stems from the ideological position of the mosaic, and it is not incidental that it makes more than one reference to the multicultural nature of Canadian society. Proponents of this policy believe that for Canada to be truly a cultural mosaic, it must provide an educational structure that permits children to learn in their "own language." This, theoretically, is true. We have stated before that a culture cannot exist without a language of its own. The attempt to make third (heritage) languages the vehicle for a better education is one step toward establishing visible and real ethnocultural communities. But can it succeed?

The outcome of these efforts will serve as a barometer of the validity of the vision of the mosaic. Our view is that ultimately a full implementation of the policy will not succeed. A number of factors will contribute to the outcome, but primarily the result will reflect the inappropriateness of such programs for ethnic students and for ethnic communities in general. Before we finalize these conclusions, let us look at the policy itself by examining the report tabled to the board in March 1982.

The report, *Towards a Comprehensive Language Policy*,[2] suggests that the transition to teaching heritage languages would take place in two stages. During the first phase, heritage language classes would take place not after school, as they do today, but during school hours. This would mean that for almost an hour per day, a number of children would leave their regular teachers and assemble with others of similar ethnicity to study the language and culture of their heritage. In the second phase, children would begin to study other subjects, such mathematics and history, in "their ethnic language." This would mean that for many ethnic children, the chance to hear and practise English would be outside the school experience. After generating many heated debates and much bitterness, the first phase was accepted and became Toronto School Board policy.

Supporters of the heritage language policy use four basic arguments. The first is that teaching ethnic children their cultural and linguistic heritage will make them proud of their backgrounds. This will not only help them feel more positive about themselves and be healthier for it, they say, but their improved self-confidence will also enhance their learning potential. The second is that because the children will be using "their own language," they can grasp new content more readily. The third is that by learning in their heritage languages, children will be able to communicate better with their parents and grandparents. The fourth is that exposure to two or more languages will enhance their capacity for learning other languages, thus opening new possibilities for them.

Although these intentions are laudable, closer scrutiny reveals the unattainability of the goals. Proponents of this policy have not adequately considered the cultural and linguistic changes at play in immigrant communities. Again, the assumptions do not correspond to the social reality of ethnic communities. Instead, they stem from a vision, an ideological position.

Let's start with their first argument. It is undeniable that ethnic children generally suffer from lower self-esteem. In a society where they do not see reflections of themselves and where perceptions of them are generally unfavourable, this is not surprising. But would it be appropriate or useful to segregate these children for an hour or more every day, so they can feel better? They could possibly develop a more positive image of themselves and their ethnicity if they were taught in their "own language" and by a teacher of similar ethnicity. It might create a nice bubble for them where everyone is ethnically alike, but the proposal raises too many questions in our minds to be embraced without reservation.

For example, would not this almost exclusive association with students of similar ethnic backgrounds widen the gap between school and society, when the child finishes school and must enter a more ethnically diverse world? Would this not psychologically predispose ethnic students to remain even more within their own communities, where they feel more comfortable? How would they, as adults educated in this manner, feel about working with people of different ethnic backgrounds if during their formative years they had associated with others only peripherally? Would not this type of education possibly encourage ethnic chauvinism? Certainly, children must feel good about their ethnicities, and we must find ways to respond to this need, but we cannot opt for a cure that could be worse than the illness.

The second argument put forward by the supporters of this policy is that by using "their own language," ethnic children would be better able to grasp the content of various school subjects. We have already seen that the language spoken by an ethnic group is no longer the original language the immigrant has brought over. To use the standard language of their country of origin in teaching does not consider this process. It is belittling to those who may never have had an adequate knowledge of the standard language, and it is detrimental to presume the best language of an immigrant's offspring is the standard language of their former country. To claim that ethnic children would do better in school if only they were given the opportunity to use "their own language" is preposterous. It hides the fact that the language these children know best, however limited it may be, is English. Teaching the standard Italian, Ukrainian, or Polish would only emphasize the gap between what they speak at home and what they are learning in school.

Certainly, newly arrived immigrant children would be able to learn more if, during a transitional period, their own language were to be used, but this is a different situation that should not be confused with that of children from ethnic communities who are born in Canada. We should not forget that the push for teaching heritage languages during school hours, and their use as languages of instruction, has not come from recently arrived newcomers. Instead, it has come from ethnic leaders of communities past the phase of arrival and early settlement.

With regard to the third point — improving the communication between parents and their children — it is not true that teaching schoolchildren in their heritage languages will reduce barriers between parents and children. It will probably have no effect, as it is unlikely that children will learn enough of the language to be able to communicate with it effectively, and even if they did, it is very unlikely they would use the standard school version of their language at home, where their parents are likely to be speaking a hybrid version of the language, perhaps on top of a dialect. If the teaching of a standard heritage language will have any effect on the gap between ethnic children born in Canada and their parents born abroad, it will be a negative one. It will make evident to the children that their parents might not only express themselves inadequately in English but are not knowledgeable in the standard forms of their heritage language, either.

The fourth point offered to promote support for third-language instruction is that by learning their heritage languages, children will develop more facility in learning other languages, which could provide better opportunities for their future careers. This is true, but let us not forget that this program is set up and referred to as third-language instruction, meaning that school kids would be dealing with English, French, a standard heritage language, and coping also with what is spoken more often at home: a hybrid language. This would all be well and good, if they were able to process such a number of languages and forms of languages.

Another argument used by the supporters of the program, when every other claim has failed, is that there is not much to worry about, because registration in such programs is voluntary. This might be the only positive thing about it. Unfortunately, it is not as simple as it seems. Ethnic organizations and businesses in each ethnic community, whose economic and political interests depend on the existence of heritage languages and other interests directly tied to viable heritage language programs, will make sure that a good number of ethnic children attend these programs. We should not forget that for obvious reasons, the ethnic media also strongly stand behind these programs, and they have the most powerful voices in ethnic communities. By appealing to their pent-up frustrations, referring to their ethnic national pride and what may seem to be the best educational interest of their children, advocates can summon many to the call. It is not difficult, in such circumstances, to convince many people to support the policy of third-language programs. After all, history teaches us that many wars have been fought that were not in the interests of those who went willingly to fight them.

What is at stake with this heritage language policy is not the educational well-being of ethnic children, but who controls the culture of the ethnic group, and what its culture will be. Control of the culture will determine which social group will have political control over the community and which economic groups will benefit. What is often lacking when speaking of ethnic communities is consideration of the different social formations that exist within them. An ethnic community cannot be taken as a whole, with a unified view on all matters. The economic, social, and political concerns of a community don't necessarily converge. People of different economic means and classes will project different political perspectives. We should not be surprised, consequently, to find that on the question of heritage languages, divergent views exist.

For example, within the Italian-Canadian community, organizations and individuals have responded differently to the policy. While the Italian-Canadian media and some organizations, such as the Canadian Centre for Italian Culture and Education, push strongly for the policy, others do not. The ethnic media in general — and the Italian-Canadian media in particular — are, for obvious reasons, totally closed to views opposing the policy. There is also support from many of the social agencies that cater to specific ethnicities.

Contrasting those closely held views, there are numerous tacit and explicit opponents of the policy. No support has been uttered by the Canadian Italian Business and Professional Association or from the Association of Italian Canadians in the Arts. These organizations do not see their growth or general welfare as being hinged on the maintenance of the Italian language. Similarly, left-leaning organizations such as the Circolo Culturale Carlo Levi have been critical of the policy. Italian-Canadian trade unionists also have not made any statements supporting the policy. Their interest is to form cultural bonds with other ethnic and mainstream workers, as their social and political demands need to be made in conjunction with the broader society. It is obvious that if they want to succeed in their goals, there must be a shared language and a shared cultural perspective that will permit them to act in unison.

Considering the above, we can say at this point that the push for heritage languages to be part of the regular curriculum and to become the language of instruction for all subjects is not widely, fully, or totally accepted among ethnic populations. Apart from its educational merits and demerits, as we are more inclined to believe, the introduction of third languages to the curriculum relates more to protecting the welfare of certain interest groups. Organizations and individuals who stand to gain from the introduction of such programs never, or seldom, take a position regarding other educational issues facing ethnic students, of which there are many. It would seem logical to assume that they would try to deal with other educational problems facing ethnic students. For example, the problem of streaming, which channels ethnic students into non-academic disciplines, has not been addressed. They should also address the question of excessively large class sizes in some working-class areas that are home to significant numbers of ethnic students. Instead, their efforts have been directed to introducing third-language programs because they see them as producing short- and long-term gains within their section of their ethnic business activity.

These pedagogical concerns of proponents of third-language instruction in fact represent a struggle over who controls the social and political development of a community. Those who control the language and culture of a group will have hegemonic control over the community. For them to have power, the culture they propose has to be welcomed and accepted by the group as a whole.

The question here is this: What language and what culture is being advocated? We have already analyzed the issues of language and culture as they relate to ethnic groups in Canada. We have concluded that although ethnics may have different cultural behaviours, they are not able to bring their cultures to the fore, where they can live and celebrate them. We have pointed out the inseparable nature of language and culture and the difficulty of maintaining them in the Canadian social context. To overcome this problem, ethnic cultural activists have relied on cultural products and the standard languages of their ancestral countries. The introduction of heritage language education during regular school hours serves to legitimize a type of culture and language, the preservation of which, although it was a vital part of the baggage brought over by the immigrants, is no longer an immediate or compelling need for their children and grandchildren. By formally making them part of the schools' curricula, ethnics will need to contend with cultural expectations that depend on the ways and language of their former countries. This may be important to them emotionally, but it becomes less important in time, and gradually recedes until it is no more than a symbolic need.

Until now, the learning of heritage languages has been limited and voluntary. Children inclined to take classes have had the opportunity to do so after school and on weekends as part of the opportunities offered by their school boards. They could also enrol in ethnic private schools that provide heritage language instruction. By making them part of the regular school curriculum and, even more significantly, by teaching other core subjects in heritage languages, school board officials give these languages an importance and an official status they presently lack. Furthermore, it presupposes that those who will continue to shape the cultural and political character of the community will be those who are more acquainted with the culture and language of their former countries.

There is another point to make here. It would seem at first that teaching heritage languages creates an opportunity for all children to take part in the programs and ultimately to benefit from the opportunities that come with them. This is not necessarily so. Although all children would be able to enrol in courses dealing with their ethnic cultures and languages, in practice it would mainly be middle-class pupils who would be able to take full advantage. As the teaching of these languages will be carried out in the standard languages of pupils' former countries, such education is, in a sense, abstract. It relates only minimally to their lives as ethnic children. These schoolchildren would most likely, when communicating at home and with their close family associates, continue to express themselves either in English or a hybrid language. The ones who would be able to internalize what they are taught and make better use of it would be those whose parents are financially secure. They would be more likely to find positive reinforcement at home from parents who have a knowledge of their cultural history, who are fluent in the standard language of their heritage, and who are up to date on the cultural and linguistic developments of their former countries. For the sons and daughters of the majority, whose parents are focused simply on making a living and who do not have the means to provide trips to their ancestral countries, heritage courses are just another thing to put up with.

The third-language policy of the Toronto Board of Education will give some the opportunity to add another dimension to their educational experiences. More significantly, it will give them the cultural and linguistic qualifications to join the cultural elite of their ethnic communities. Offering heritage language programs to all, by holding them during regular school hours and making them the language of instruction, will aid in the formation and the perpetuation of the ethnic mosaic. It will help some people become leaders of their particular pieces of the mosaic, but it does not offer the same potential to all. These programs do not serve the pedagogical benefit of most ethnic children. The institutionalization of these programs is not organically linked to the development of the ethnic community. Instead, they represent an imposition by a sector of the community that tries to become the cultural and political ethnic elite.

We have attempted to prove that introducing third-language public instruction in Toronto is not pedagogically beneficial to the vast majority of ethnic students. We have focused on third-language instruction because it is emblematic of the policy of multiculturalism and its metaphoric corollary, the mosaic. It illustrates the idealistic nature of the policy along with its inherent contradictions. The policy cannot possibly improve the educational welfare of ethnic students because its assumptions do not correspond to their social and cultural reality. In fact, we feel strongly that third-language instruction is contrary to their educational and overall well-being.

Conclusion

The policy of multiculturalism, passed in 1971, was the response of Pierre Elliot Trudeau's Liberal government to a number of issues, and touched on many unresolved questions about Canadian society. Since the Second World War, Canada's economy had been expanding rapidly, creating a huge need for immigrants to facilitate growth, including building the infrastructure to enable that growth. Meeting new social and political needs demanded a social and cultural transformation. Further, Canada had yet to come to grips with issues that history had left festering: debts still owed to the Native population, a colonial heritage to be properly recognized and managed, and not-so-"quiet" dissent in Quebec. In essence, in 1971 Canada was still very much a nation in the making, with significant matters to be sorted and a need for new political directives to shape socio-cultural change.

Such important questions required careful attention and political initiative, including a national inquiry to analyze the social forces at play. The Royal Commission on Bilingualism and Biculturalism was set in 1963 and finished its work in 1967. In time, the policy of multiculturalism was created and adopted. The policy used the Commission's report as a foundation for navigating the issue of integrating the "other." Although the policy mainly

CONCLUSION

followed the framework set out by the commissioners, the government excluded or changed some of the Commission's original terms
of reference, which had set directives and limits for the subjects at
hand. The terms of reference were critical and altering them mud-
died the policy's objectives for integrating the "other" into the fabric
of Canadian culture. The policy does not consider the meaning of
culture as it relates to ethnicity in Canada. It does not deal with the
process of integrating and preserving various cultures, nor does it
lay out who the "others" really are.

To the commissioners, it was clear the terms represented a point
of view, an ideological perspective. Removing them would permit
an ideological stance that could theoretically run contrary to the
essence of Canada's historical and social reality. To them it had
been clear the English and French were the founding peoples of
Canada's nationhood. Native populations were distinct as "the first
inhabitants of this country," and the ethnic population comprised
all those "who came to Canada during or after the founding of the
Canadian state." Along with the clarifications of those terms, the
commissioners had also specified that a person's ethnicity is not
determined objectively. Rather, it is subjective, and not dependent
on a person's last name.

The policy of multiculturalism incorporates the issues the commissioners saw as important, but by excluding the terms of reference, or harbingers, the policy lacks direction. The Commission had
been quite clear about using harbingers that recognized Canada's
historical reality to delineate its work. The policy-makers were indifferent and oblivious to those signposts, allowing historical realities and social developments to remain hidden or unclear.

Without such terms of reference, the policy of multiculturalism
became ambiguous with respect to ethnicity and culture, allowing politicians and others to bend it to suit their views and interests regarding
the integration of "others" into Canada's social and cultural fabric.

The changes do not bode well for clarifying the process of integration and how ethnics would fare. The policy has made it difficult for people in Canada to know who are immigrants and who are not, who are ethnics and who are not, and which cultural values of ethnics are to be respected and which values of the larger society the newcomers need to adopt. Contrary to its stated purpose, it has created social unease, confusion, and ambiguity.

The policy is a political answer to some problems of the country. It addresses Native issues and those of ethnic populations but leaves unresolved the divisive issues of French-Canadian identity and political developments in Quebec. The policy tries to make amends to the Natives, appease the French, and provide some assistance to newcomers, but the ambiguity of the policy has sown broader apprehension and confusion. As always, confusion breeds error.

From this context of multiple issues and considerable ambiguity on some of the policy's cardinal points, the theory of the ethnic mosaic surfaced. We have studied the construction of this theory and found that its assumptions are mistaken. Its understanding of culture and language is incorrect and misleading. We have also affirmed that culture is not primordial but situational, and that culture and language cannot be separated.

Ideologists of the ethnic mosaic make assumptions about ethnic group formations that do not correspond to any sociological determining factors, and do not reflect social ethnic-group realities as they exist in Canada. Further, their views on immigration and immigrants follow the same erroneous path, superficially assuming that everyone in Canada is an immigrant or a descendant of an immigrant.

Removing the terms of reference has muddled the policy and rendered it ambiguous. This ambiguity has permitted the development of the theory of the ethnic mosaic and its by-product, the ideology of the ethnic mosaic. Ideologies cultivate passions, and history has shown how ideologies that do not correspond to social realities can lead to catastrophic results. Our unfavourable opinion of the theory of the mosaic and its corresponding ideology has not been reached a priori. We have deconstructed and analyzed their underpinnings and concluded they cannot serve their intended purposes of integrating Canada's ethnic populations and, if pursued, could generate unpleasant social repercussions.

An ideology unto itself is innocuous. Like a weapon, if it is not used, it can never do any good or any harm, but the ideology of the mosaic is not idle. It has generated heated public discussion, political debate, academic analysis and, most significantly, social activism, by both those who promote its social benefits and opponents who consider it harmful — even dangerous. With this book, we are continuing this discussion while we wait for ideologically motivated policies, recently legislated, to verify the validity of our position. In these pages we have also stated that the validity of an ideology can be proven only by its social application. That rule certainly applies here.

In our analysis of the theory of the ethnic mosaic and the policy of multiculturalism, in the construct of the mosaic we have also uncovered a major flaw that, had it been considered earlier, would have rendered its formation impossible. It is the social development, right here in Canada, of a sizable population not confined or defined by ethnicity, cultural heritage, or linguistic requirements. It consists of unhyphenated Canadians we can call "mainstream," for lack of a better term. It is not a true group because it does not socialize as such and is not even an aggregation. This population is composed of people who correspond ethnically to what their Canadian passports state: Canadian. Whatever the appropriate term could be — mainstream, assemblage, melting cauldron, or melting pot — we need to acknowledge these unhyphenated Canadians.

This mainstream is a result of people settling in Canada. Regardless of whether they are descendants of early French and

English settlers or not, the fact is they have become Canadians. It is an indisputable fact that when people of different cultural behaviours come together, they create new forms of communication: a culture, a way of life that distinguishes them. It is a process of sociality, a human characteristic stronger than social barriers erected to prevent it, and it is not exclusive to Canada. It has happened in the United States, Mexico, and Argentina, and it is happening similarly in Australia. It happens in countries where an infusion of the "other" has taken place, and it will continue to happen in Canada. The Canadian mainstream will continue to develop, and hyphenated Canadians will recede despite manufactured social barriers.

The barriers recall the Daughters of the Empire, determined to prevent this sort of general grouping of people. They had a vision of what being Canadian should be, definitely not what they would see today. They erected socio-cultural barriers using theories about assimilation to prevent contagion, to stop the "other" from being equal, to avert the sociality of humans. Nonetheless, the pressure to assimilate has psychologically damaged many on both sides of the barriers, hindering Canada's coming of age. The end of it all is that Canadian society is having the last word on this: the voice of the bigoted has not been followed. Sooner or later those views merit ridicule, defeat, and historical disgrace.

What's baffling is that this mainstream identity has developed and grown in Canadian society without being recognized as having its own sociological attributes, and that it is hardly even acknowledged. Among all the willing acceptance and eager discussions about the Canadian mosaic, very little is being said about the Canadian mainstream. Although the results of official surveys about Canadian ethnicity show that most people identify themselves as plainly Canadian, the results have not prompted much analysis. These responses strongly suggest that much of the population defines its own ethnicity subjectively, and not by the last names they carry. Even in the face of strong evidence to the contrary, the idea that Canada is an ethnic mosaic somehow prevails.

Regardless of what logic dictates and studies affirm, there is a denial — or at least a concealment — of the mainstream. We are not here to discuss why this happens, but to show that it does. We could form opinions and work to support a hypothesis about the cause, but there is no research-based information to use in forming an argument. However, it is possible to think that if the ill-suited framework of the ethnic mosaic becomes socially operable and finds some success, as the ideologists of the theory aspire, it would clearly benefit today's elite groups. Obscuring the existence of a social reality — in this case, the mainstream social formation — follows the self-serving tactics of elites. In our case, the Canadian one, that would mean purporting to make changes while working to keep things as they are. A tactic for maintaining the status quo is to fend off change by obscuring other possibilities.

Obviously, at the time of the Commission's report, and at the time the policy of multiculturalism was passed, the explosive issue of Quebec nationalism was foremost in the prime minister's mind. The political brilliance of the entire policy was that its actual objective was to neutralize the messy identity issues of French-Canadians, Natives, and some ethnic communities, by levelling all their cultural rights. Canada would be multicultural, with all having the same cultural rights, but officially, only the French would have their language recognized, even though the commissioners had stated that the separation of language and culture was not possible and that one is a factor of the other. In the process, Canada becomes bilingual but simultaneously multicultural. Tactically, it appears the government hoped that this recognition would quell the Quebecois turmoil, that Natives would accept some more poor lands and some money to do "their thing," and the ethnics would be satisfied with some podiums and a little money to do theirs.

That the elites of Canadian society would welcome the chance to define the country as a mosaic is hardly surprising, because setting the social structure of society as a series of connected islands could serve them quite well. They would remain as elites within their piece of the mosaic while the rest of the people would happily locate themselves in other, less influential but still protected parts of the social formation. As cynical as it may have been, it was also a clever idea. In his book *The Vertical Mosaic*, John Porter shows that the Canadian elite is essentially made up of English-Canadians. We have also shown that this elite is being penetrated by Canadians of other ethnicities. If the mosaic model could be made to work, it could keep those "others" at bay.

Fortunately, things do not function as neatly as some would like. Elites have always existed, but their membership does change. Just as empires rise and fall, so do elites. It is the dynamics of people working and playing together in the practical, everyday world that creates ferment and, as we know, fermentation causes change.

We have pointed out in our analysis of the theory of the ethnic mosaic and its corresponding ideology that the assumptions on which they are based are incorrect. We are already seeing that some policies and proposals flowing from the ideology of the ethnic mosaic have not been received well. Some have triggered polemical confrontations. The Natives, the Quebecois, and the Acadians do not see their groups as equal to all the rest. They have seen proposals relating to them as contrary to the history of the country, to their vision of themselves, and to their place in Canada.

We have seen how the ambiguous nature of the policy of multiculturalism has fostered different and conflicting interpretations. Native populations of Canada, French-Canadians, and Acadians have rejected being placed on an equal footing with those who came to settle much later in Canada.

CONCLUSION

The ethnic groups' response to the policy was generally favourable at first, and while it still well regarded in some parts of some ethnic communities, it is fading in others and there is open opposition to some projects emanating from the ethnic mosaic concept. Ethnic communities, like other communities, are developing economically and professionally, and socially becoming stratified and diversified. The varied responses to the policy reflect that. As with any political policy, support and opposition relate to economic and socio-cultural interests.

This is no more evident than with the introduction of the heritage language policy by the Toronto School Board. As we write, the policy is being presented to the Board, where it appears to have enough support to be passed. This policy has been widely discussed and debated during the school board election campaign, where it has been tackled from all sides. The future of this policy is still to be seen, and many fear where it might lead. The second phase of the policy, which would segregate children according to the languages of their heritage, seems unlikely to materialize, but that remains to be seen.

The point here is that the ideology of the mosaic is passing from concept to praxis and creating disjunction and discord in the process, including direct opposition to the vision of the ethnic mosaic itself. We have also pointed out that the policy of multiculturalism is ambiguous and muddled, and when used as a political tool to project mosaic-like communities, it is rejected. Native people and French-speaking Canadians reject the policy forcefully, while mainstream Canadians either reject it or are indifferent. There is obviously a link between the policy, the theory of the mosaic, and the ideology of the mosaic. The hostility and indifference are not directed toward the policy itself, nor its idealism, but toward the vision of the ethnic mosaic. The School Board policy on heritage languages is an example of how this is playing out. As we have shown, at best it may be innocuous, but if fully adopted, it could have serious and negative repercussions for our society.

It's important here to restate that the commissioners viewed immigrants — the ethnics — as having cultural values similar to those of their receiving country. The essence of Canadian society — its cultural base, its constitutional principles — is not in question. It is acknowledged, accepted, and rightly demanded to be respected by the Canadian government when immigrants seek entry. The music we listen to, the clothing we wear, the food we eat, and the movies we watch are some of the positive ways we express and assert our cultural differences. They give rise to the quest for fair, humane, practical, and clearly defined models of integration.

The cultural struggle of immigrants who settle in a new home is not easy. It is a sort of psychological battle, sometimes between their competing selves, sometimes with others of their own ethnicity, and sometimes with the wider national community. They need to adapt to Canadian society while maintaining their cultural identities, originated and formed in different settings. It is difficult for them to balance entrenched cultural values based on other circumstances with the values and circumstances of their new lives. The values they bring are static, while the new values continue to evolve, demanding attention, acceptance, and incorporation. The new ways are fierce, impetuous, and multifaceted. They hammer constantly, weakening the wrinkled cultural shield of the old.

It is not our goal here to advance an alternative to the ethnic mosaic ideology, but we would like to suggest the spirit in which ethnic populations and Canadian society at large can approach a more effective and successful process for integration. We need to combine the needs and desires of people who feel they are and behave culturally as ethnics, while keeping in mind the interests of the wider society. The model of the mosaic is not appropriate or helpful for building Canada. We need and want to integrate, not segregate. We want to acknowledge and accept the basic *raison d'être* of Canadian society, but we also want the Canadian experience to include elements of other cultures. We want newcomers to be included, respected, and recognized for their contributions to Canadian society, including its economy, and its social and cultural fabric.

Social policies, particularly schools' curricula, should be formulated and implemented with the interests of all schoolchildren in mind. We need to safeguard the pedagogical welfare of ethnic pupils. Their ethnicity should be considered respectfully, and their cultural backgrounds ought to be integral to every child's education. All of society, but especially educators, should be informed explicitly and directly about the importance of immigration to this country, and understand why Canada has deliberately sought immigrants to further its progress. We need to unite in this endeavor, to share our cultures with one another and with all Canadians. We want our society to include the cultures of the "others," and to be as multicultural as possible within the parameters clearly defined by the Royal Commission, rather than by generalized statements that have little practical application and signify nothing.

Bibliography

Anderson, Alan B. "Ukrainian Ethnicity: Generations and Change in Rural Saskatchewan." In *Two Nations, Many Cultures: Ethnic Groups in Canada*, edited by Jean Leonard Elliott, 250–69. Toronto: Prentice-Hall of Canada, 1979.

Avery, Donald. *Dangerous Foreigners: European Immigrant Workers and Labour Radicalism in Canada, 1896–1932*. Toronto: McClelland and Stewart, 1979.

Bancroft, George. *Outreach for Understanding: A Report on Intercultural Seminars*. Toronto: Ontario Ministry of Culture and Recreation, 1976.

Bégin, Monique. *Multiculturalism as State Policy; Second Canadian Conference on Multiculturalism*. Ottawa: Supply and Services Canada, 1976: 4–5.

Berry, John W., Rudolf Kalin, and Donald M. Taylor. *Multiculturalism and Ethnic Attitudes in Canada*. Ottawa: Minister of Supply and Services, 1977.

Bianco, Carla. *The Two Rosetos*. Bloomington, IN: Indiana University Press, 1974.

Breton, Raymond. "Institutional Completeness of Ethnic Communities and the Personal Relations of Immigrants." *American Journal of Sociology* 70, no. 2 (1964): 193–205

Brotz, Howard. "Multiculturalism in Canada: A Muddle." *Canadian Public Policy* 6, no. 1 (Winter 1980): 41–46.

Brown, Rosemary. "Presentation by R. Brown." *Multiculturalism as State Policy; Second Canadian Conference on Multiculturalism*. Ottawa: Supply and Services Canada, 1976: 7–10.

Caccia, Charles (1973, 30 May). "Multiculturalism." Canada. Parliament. House of Commons. *Edited Hansard*. 29th Parliament, 1st Session. lipad.ca/full/permalink/2855781/.

Canadian Institute of Cultural Research. *Change of Name*. Toronto: Canadian Institute of Cultural Research, 1965.

Connor, Ralph. *The Foreigner: A Tale of Saskatchewan*. Waterloo, Ontario: Wilfred Laurier University Press, 2014 (originally published 1909).

Cummins, Jim, and Harold Troper. "Multiculturalism and Language Policy in Canada." In *Language Policy in Canada: Current Issues*, edited by Juan Cobarrubias, 16–27. Quebec: International Center for Research on Bilingualism, 1985.

Davidson Dunton, A., and Jean-Louis Gagnon. *Report of the Royal Commission on Bilingualism and Biculturalism. Book IV: The Cultural Contribution of the Other Ethnic Groups*. Ottawa: Privy Council Office of Canada, 1970. publications.gc.ca/collections/collection_2014/bcp-pco/Z1-1963-1-5-4-2-eng.pdf.

Driedger, Leo. *The Canadian Ethnic Mosaic*. Toronto: McClelland and Stewart, 1978.

Elliott, Jean Leonard, and Augie Fleras. *Unequal Relations: An Introduction to Race, Ethnic and Aboriginal Dynamics in Canada*. United Kingdom: Prentice Hall Allyn and Bacon Canada, 1999.

Gallo, Patrick J. *Ethnic Alienation: The Italian-Americans*. Rutherford, N.J.: Fairleigh Dickinson Press, 1974.

Gans, Herbert J. "Symbolic Ethnicity: The Future of Ethnic Groups and Cultures in America." *Ethnic and Racial Studies* 2, no. 1 (1979): 1–20.

Gordon, Milton. *Assimilation in American Life*. New York: Oxford University Press, 1964.

Johnson, Graham E. "Chinese Canadians in the '70s: New Wine in New Bottles." In *Two Nations, Many Cultures: Ethnic Groups in Canada*, edited by Jean Leonard Elliott, 393–411. Toronto: Prentice-Hall of Canada, 1979.

Kallen, Horace. *Culture and Democracy in the United States*. New York: Bonin and Livewright, 1924.

Mallea, John R., and Jonathan C. Young. *Cultural Diversity and Canadian Education: Issues and Innovations*. Ottawa: Carleton University Press, 1984.

Marlyn, John. *Under the Ribs of Death*. Toronto: McClelland and Stewart, 1971.

Matejko, Alexander J. "Multiculturalism: The Polish Canadian Case." In *Two Nations, Many Cultures: Ethnic Groups in Canada*, edited by Jean Leonard Elliott, 237–49. Toronto: Prentice-Hall of Canada, 1979.

McCormack, Ross. "Cloth Caps and Jobs: The Ethnicity of English Immigrants in Canada, 1900–1914." In *Ethnicity, Power and Politics in Canada*, edited by Jorgen Dahlie and Tina Fernando, 38–57. Toronto: Methuen, 1981.

McKay, James. "An Exploratory Synthesis of Primordial and Mobilizationist Approaches to Ethnic Phenomena." *Ethnic and Racial Studies* 5, no. 4 (1982): 395–420.

McKay, James, and French L. Sewins. "Ethnicity and Ethnic Group: A Conceptual Analysis and Reformation." *Ethnic and Racial Studies* 1, no. 4 (1978), 265–85.

Moodley, Koogila. "Canadian Multiculturalism as Ideology." *Ethnic and Racial Studies* 6, no. 3 (1983): 320–31.

Nagata, Judith A. "One Vine, Many Branches: Internal Differentiation in Canadian Ethnic Groups." In *Two Nations, Many Cultures: Ethnic Groups in Canada*, edited by Jean Leonard Elliott, 173–181. Toronto: Prentice-Hall of Canada, 1979.

Office of the Commissioner of Official Languages. 1963. "Prime Minister Lester B. Pearson Establishes the Royal Commission on Bilingualism and Biculturalism."

Porter, John. *The Vertical Mosaic: An Analysis of Social Class and Power in Canada*. Toronto: University of Toronto Press, 1965.

Reitz, Jeffrey G. *The Survival of Ethnic Groups*. Toronto: McGraw-Hill Ryerson, 1980.

Roberts, Lance W., and Clifton, Rodney A. "Exploring the Ideology of Canadian Multiculturalism." *Canadian Public Policy* 8, no. 1 (1982): 88–94.

Robinson, Ira. *A History of Antisemitism in Canada*. Waterloo: Wilfrid Laurier University Press, 2015.

Ryan, Claude. "Canada: Bicultural or Multicultural?" In *Immigration and the Rise of Multiculturalism*, edited by Howard Palmer, 147–50. Toronto: Copp Clark Publishing, 1975.

Ryerson, A.E. "The Importance of Education to a Manufacturing and a Free People." *Journal of Education for Upper Canada* 1, no. 10 (1848): 290–320.

Smith, M.G. "Ethnicity and Ethnic Groups in America: The View from Harvard." *Ethnic and Racial Studies* 5, no. 1 (1982): 1–22.

Toronto Board of Education. *The Bias of Culture: An Issue Paper on Multiculturalism*. Toronto: The Board of Education for the City of Toronto, 1975.

——. *Towards a Comprehensive Language Policy: Final Report of the Work Group on Third Language Instruction*. Toronto: The Board of Education for the City of Toronto, March 1982.

Trudeau, Pierre (1971, October 8). "Announcement of Implementation of Policy of Multiculturalism Within Bilingual Framework."

Canada. Parliament. House of Commons. *Edited Hansard.* 28th Parliament, 3rd Session. lipad.ca/full/permalink/2756565/.

Tylor, Edward B. *Primitive Culture: Researches into the Development of Mythology, Philosophy, Religion, Art, and Custom.* London: John Murray, 1871.

White, Naomi R. 1978. "Ethnicity, Culture and Pluralism." *Ethnicity and Racial Studies* 1 (2):139–53.

Yinger, J. Milton. "Toward a Theory of Assimilation and Dissimilation." *Ethnic and Racial Studies* 4, no. 3 (1961): 249–64.

Notes

Chapter 1: The Social Integration of Newcomers to Canada

1   Donald Avery, *Dangerous Foreigners: European Immigrant Workers and Labour Radicalism in Canada, 1896–1932* (Toronto: McClelland and Stewart, 1979), 15.

2   Cited in Jean Leonard Elliott and Augie Fleras, *Unequal Relations: An Introduction to Race, Ethnic, and Aboriginal Dynamics in Canada* (Waterloo, ON: Wilfrid Laurier University Press, 2015), 21.

3   Cited in Ira Robinson, *A History of Antisemitism in Canada* (Waterloo, ON: Wilfrid Laurier University Press, 2015), 63.

4   Cited in John R. Mallea and Jonathan C. Young, *Cultural Diversity and Canadian Education: Issues and Innovations* (Ottawa: Carleton University Press, 1984), 27.

5   John Marlyn, *Under the Ribs of Death* (Toronto: McClelland and Stewart, 1971), 24.

6   Canadian Institute of Cultural Research, *Change of Name* (Toronto: Canadian Institute of Cultural Research, 1965).

7   Ibid.

8   Ibid.

9   Jim Cummins and Harold Troper, "Multiculturalism and Language Policy in Canada," in *Language Policy in Canada: Current Issues*, ed. Juan Cobarrubias (Quebec: International Center for Research on Bilingualism, 1985): 17.

10   Ralph Connor, *The Foreigner: A Tale of Saskatchewan* (Waterloo, Ontario: Wilfred Laurier University Press, originally published 1909), 5.

11   Horace Kallen, *Culture and Democracy in the United States* (New York: Bonin and Livewright, 1924), 217.

12   Kallen, *Culture and Democracy*, 254.

13   Milton Gordon, *Assimilation in American Life* (New York: Oxford University Press, 1964), 148.

14 Gordon, *Assimilation*, 149.
15 Edward Burnett Tylor, *Primitive Culture: Researches into the Development of Mythology, Philosophy, Religion, Art, and Custom* (London: John Murray, 1871), 1.
16 Howard Brotz, "Multiculturalism in Canada: A Muddle," *Canadian Public Policy 6*, no. 1 (1980).
17 A. Davidson Dunton and Jean-Louis Gagnon, *Report of the Royal Commission on Bilingualism and Biculturalism. Book IV: The Cultural Contribution of the Other Ethnic Groups* (Ottawa: Privy Council Office of Canada, 1970), 173.
18 John Porter, *The Vertical Mosaic: An Analysis of Social Class and Power in Canada* (Toronto: University of Toronto Press, 1965), 64.

Chapter 2: The Royal Commission and the Resulting Policy of Multiculturalism

1 Office of the Commissioner of Official Languages. 1963. "Prime Minister Lester B. Pearson Establishes the Royal Commission on Bilingualism and Biculturalism."
2 Davidson Dunton and Gagnon, *Report of the RCBB Book IV*, 228.
3 Davidson Dunton and Gagnon, *Report of the RCBB Book IV*, 229.
4 Ibid.
5 Davidson Dunton and Gagnon, *Report of the RCBB Book IV*, 220.
6 Davidson Dunton and Gagnon, *Report of the RCCB Book IV*, xxiii.
7 Mallea and Young, *Cultural Diversity*, 106.
8 Davidson Dunton and Gagnon, *Report of the RCCB Book IV*, xxii.
9 Davidson Dunton and Gagnon, *Report of the RCCB Book IV*, xxiii.
10 Davidson Dunton and Gagnon, *Report of the RCCB Book IV*, xxvi.
11 Davidson Dunton and Gagnon, *Report of the RCCB Book IV*, 13.
12 Pierre Trudeau (1971, October 8). "Announcement of Implementation of Policy of Multiculturalism Within Bilingual Framework." Canada. Parliament. House of Commons. *Edited Hansard.* 28th Parliament, 3rd Session.
13 Ibid.
14 Monique Bégin, *Multiculturalism as State Policy; Second Canadian Conference on Multiculturalism* (Ottawa: Supply and Services Canada, 1976): 4–5.
15 Brotz, "Multiculturalism in Canada: A Muddle."
16 Moodley, Kogila. "Canadian Multiculturalism as Ideology." *Ethnic and Racial Studies 6*, no. 3 (1983): 326.

17 Bégin, *Second Canadian Conference on Multiculturalism*.
18 Bégin, *Second Canadian Conference on Multiculturalism*.

Chapter 3: The Ideology of the Mosaic

1 Leo Driedger, *The Canadian Ethnic Mosaic* (Toronto: McClelland and Stewart, 1978).
2 Porter, *Vertical Mosaic*.

Chapter 4: The Assumption of Immigration

1 John W. Berry, Rudolf Kalin, and Donald M. Taylor, *Multiculturalism and Ethnic Attitudes in Canada* (Ottawa: Minister of Supply and Services, 1977).
2 Rosemary Brown, *Multiculturalism as State Policy; Second Canadian Conference on Multiculturalism* (Ottawa: Supply and Services Canada, 1976): 7.
3 Charles Caccia (1973, 30 May), "Multiculturalism," Canada. Parliament. House of Commons. *Edited Hansard*. 29th Parliament, 1st Session.

Chapter 5: Assumptions About Ethnicity

1 James McKay, "An Exploratory Synthesis of Primordial and Mobilizationist Approaches to Ethnic Phenomena," *Ethnic and Racial Studies* 5, no. 4 (1982): 398.
2 M.G. Smith, "Ethnicity and Ethnic Groups in America: The View from Harvard," *Ethnic and Racial Studies* 5, no. 1 (1982): 6.
3 Ibid.
4 The approach taken here, to distinguish between an ethnic category and an ethnic group, is based largely upon an article by James McKay and French L. Sewins from the Australian National University in 1978: "Ethnicity and Ethnic Group: A Conceptual Analysis and Reformation," *Ethnic and Racial Studies* 1, no. 4 (1978), 265–85.
5 Raymond Breton, "Institutional Completeness of Ethnic Communities and the Personal Relations of Immigrants," *American Journal of Sociology* 70, no. 2 (1964): 193–205.
6 The situation is different for French-Canadians outside Quebec. We will not enter into a discussion of their rights and whether they are similar to those of the other ethnic groups. However, it does

seem that although historically, these people differ from other ethnics, when we consider other factors, they are not different. A general statement is not possible here and each French-Canadian community outside Quebec would need to be looked at its own merit to determine to what degree they are an ethnic group or whether they could be considered a national ethnic group.

7   Jeffrey G. Reitz, *The Survival of Ethnic Groups* (Toronto: McGraw-Hill Ryerson, 1980).

Chapter 6: Mainstream Canadians

1   Berry, Kalin, and Taylor, *Multiculturalism and Ethnic Attitudes.*
2   Toronto Board of Education, *The Bias of Culture: An Issue Paper on Multiculturalism* (Toronto: The Board of Education for the City of Toronto, 1975).
3   Ross McCormack, "Cloth Caps and Jobs: The Ethnicity of English Immigrants in Canada, 1900–1914," in *Ethnicity, Power and Politics in Canada*, ed. Jorgen Dahlie and Tina Fernando (Toronto: Methuen, 1981), 38.

Chapter 7: The Assumption of Culture

1   Driedger, *Canadian Ethnic Mosaic*, 11.
2   Naomi R. White, "Ethnicity, Culture and Pluralism," *Ethnicity and Racial Studies* 1, no. 2 (1978): 142.
3   Brotz, "Multiculturalism in Canada: A Muddle."
4   Tylor, *Primitive Culture.*
5   Brotz, "Multiculturalism in Canada: A Muddle."

Chapter 8: Acculturation

1   J. Milton Yinger, "Toward a Theory of Assimilation and Dissimilation," *Ethnic and Racial Studies* 4, no. 3 (1961): 251.
2   Gordon, *Assimilation in American Life.*
3   Carla Bianco, *The Two Rosetos* (Bloomington, IN: Indiana University Press, 1974).
4   Patrick J. Gallo, *Ethnic Alienation: The Italian-Americans* (Rutherford, N.J: Fairleigh Dickinson Press, 1974).
5   Alan B. Anderson, "Ukrainian Ethnicity: Generations and Change in Rural Saskatchewan," in *Two Nations, Many Cultures: Ethnic*

Groups in Canada, ed. Jean Leonard Elliott (Toronto: Prentice-Hall of Canada, 1979), 259.

6   Alexander J. Matejko, "Multiculturalism: The Polish Canadian Case," in *Two Nations, Many Cultures: Ethnic Groups in Canada*, ed. Jean Leonard Elliott (Toronto: Prentice-Hall of Canada, 1979), 243.

7   Anderson, "Ukrainian Ethnicity," 259.

8   Moodley, "Canadian Multiculturalism as Ideology."

9   Anderson, "Ukrainian Ethnicity," 250.

10 Ibid.

11 Graham E. Johnson, "Chinese Canadians in the '70s: New Wine in New Bottles," in *Two Nations, Many Cultures: Ethnic Groups in Canada*, ed. Jean Leonard Elliott (Toronto: Prentice-Hall of Canada, 1983), 401.

12 Herbert J. Gans, "Symbolic Ethnicity: The Future of Ethnic Groups and Cultures in America," *Ethnic and Racial Studies* 2, no. 1 (1979): 13.

13 Matejko, "Multiculturalism: The Polish Canadian Case."

14 John Porter, *Vertical Mosaic*.

15 Ibid.

16 White, "Ethnicity, Culture and Pluralism," 142.

17 White, "Ethnicity, Culture and Pluralism," 146.

18 Anderson, "Ukrainian Ethnicity."

19 Matejko, "Multiculturalism: The Polish Canadian Case," 237.

20 Lance W. Roberts and Rodney A. Clifton, "Exploring the Ideology of Canadian Multiculturalism," *Canadian Public Policy* 8, no. 1 (1982): 88–94.

21 Gans, "Symbolic Ethnicity," 1.

22 Gans, "Symbolic Ethnicity," 9.

23 Gans, "Symbolic Ethnicity," 6.

24 Gans, "Symbolic Ethnicity," 9.

25 Matejko, "Multiculturalism: The Polish Canadian Case," 242.

26 Anderson, "Ukrainian Ethnicity."

27 Judith A. Nagata, "One Vine, Many Branches: Internal Differentiation in Canadian Ethnic Groups," in *Two Nations, Many Cultures: Ethnic Groups in Canada*, ed. Jean Leonard Elliott (Toronto: Prentice-Hall of Canada, 1979), 180.

Chapter 9: Canadian Mainstream Culture

1   Yinger, "Assimilation and Dissimilation," 251.

2   George Bancroft, *Outreach for Understanding: A Report on Intercultural Seminars* (Toronto: Ontario Ministry of Culture and Recreation, 1976), 19.
3   A.E. Ryerson, "The Importance of Education to a Manufacturing and a Free People," *Journal of Education for Upper Canada* 1, no. 10 (1848) 290–320.

Chapter 10: The Adverse Effects of the Ideology of the Mosaic

1   Claude Ryan, "Canada: Bicultural or Multicultural?" in *Immigration and the Rise of Multiculturalism*, ed. Howard Palmer (Toronto: Copp Clark Publishing, 1975), 150.
2   Toronto Board of Education, March 1982, *Towards a Comprehensive Language Policy: Final Report of the Work Group on Third Language Instruction* (Toronto, Ontario: Toronto Board of Education).